A
World
Challenged

A
World
Challenged

*Fighting Terrorism in
the Twenty-First Century*

Yevgeny M. Primakov

THE NIXON CENTER
and
BROOKINGS INSTITUTION PRESS
Washington, D.C.

Copyright © 2004
Yevgeny M. Primakov

Library of Congress Cataloging-in-Publication data

Primakov, E. M. (Evgeniæi Maksimovich)
   A world challenged : fighting terrorism in the twenty-first century /
Yevgeny M. Primakov.
      p.   cm.
Includes bibliographical references and index.
   ISBN 0-8157-7194-0 (cloth : alk. paper)
   1. Terrorism. 2. Terrorism—Prevention. I. Title.
HV6431.P74 2004
363.32—dc22   2003023943

9 8 7 6 5 4 3 2 1

The paper used in this publication meets minimum requirements of the American National Standard for Information Sciences—Permanence of Paper for Printed Library Materials: ANSI Z39.48-1992.

Typeset in Minion

Composition by Cynthia Stock
Silver Spring, Maryland

Printed by R. R. Donnelley
Harrisonburg, Virginia

CONTENTS

FOREWORD *by Henry A. Kissinger*   vii

1 TERRORISM: A TERRIBLE FORCE UNLEASED
   ON THE WORLD   1

2 THE AGGRESSION OF ISLAM: TRUTH OR FICTION?   20

3 PEACE IN THE MIDDLE EAST: A NEW APPROACH
   IS NEEDED   31

4 THE U.S. WAR ON TERROR   59

5 CENTERS OF POWER: ONE OR MANY?   94

6 LESSONS FOR ALL   102

7 RUSSIA'S ROLE IN THE CONTEMPORARY WORLD   113

NOTES   137

INDEX   141

Foreword

Yevgeny Primakov's new book, *A World Challenged,* makes an important contribution to understanding how Moscow views its role in this new international environment. One need not agree with everything Primakov writes—and I don't—to appreciate the significance and weight of his perspective.

First, Primakov is an experienced and astute observer of the international arena. He has served variously as an influential journalist, a prominent academic and think tank director, the chairman of the upper house of the Soviet parliament, the director of the Soviet and Russian foreign intelligence services, and ultimately, foreign minister and prime minister under Boris Yeltsin. In these many roles he has developed a broad network of connections from New York to London to Baghdad and Kabul. He has observed and participated in major global developments for over forty years. Whatever one thinks of his views, he has been an enlightened academic and a serious and pragmatic official.

And Primakov remains an important presence in current Russian politics, through his roles as chairman of the Chamber of Commerce and Industry, a Russian business association, and as an informal adviser to current Russian President Vladimir Putin. His world view clearly reflects mainstream Russian thinking—with all its complexities—on Russia's place in the twenty-first-century international system. This thinking is not always well understood outside Russia, and some of its elements are clearly not in full alignment with American interests and values. But so long as Russia remains a serious power that can affect vital U.S. objectives in areas such as the war on terrorism and nonproliferation, Russian views do matter and should be understood and, where appropriate, taken into account in order to make American foreign policy more effective.

HENRY A. KISSINGER
Honorary Chairman
The Nixon Center

A
World
Challenged

1

TERRORISM: A TERRIBLE FORCE UNLEASHED ON THE WORLD

It is a horrific sight. September 11, 2001. CNN Live is showing amateur video of an airliner slicing into one of the World Trade Center's Twin Towers, the commercial heart of New York City. The broadcast was replayed around the globe. Before people could begin to make sense of what they were seeing—like most, my first thought had been that it was some kind of terrible air disaster—we heard the shocked voice of a commentator shouting, "A second plane has hit the other tower!" The world witnessed flames erupting and flowing across the building's facade. As one tower became gray from smoke and soot, the first crumbled to the ground. Thousands of people in the towers that morning perished.

Simultaneously, yet another plane slammed into the Pentagon, in Arlington, Virginia, and a fourth plane hijacked by terrorists crashed in Pennsylvania without reaching its target—probably the White House or the Capitol in Washington, D.C.

It was the most significant terrorist act in history. In the immediate aftermath of the tragedies, most if not all clear-thinking people were naturally seized by grief and compassion for the Americans as they coped with their losses, and they felt only rage toward the monsters who had perpetrated this horror. Yet the painful emotional shock has begun to heal, and now the time has come for thoughtful reflection. Careful analysis is crucial, for the events of September 11 have begun to proliferate. The signature form of mass-casualty suicide terrorism has surfaced elsewhere, such as in Bali, Indonesia, where a criminal act claimed two hundred lives. Another link in this chain was perpetrated when terrorists took eight hundred hostages in Moscow on October 25, 2002, and prepared to execute them. A Russian special forces unit brilliantly thwarted the attempt, but more than one hundred people still lost their lives.

From Regicide to Mass Acts of Terrorism

Many equate any violent act that is inappropriate or "out of place" with terrorism. In reality, terrorism is a specific form of political activity that seeks to achieve its ends by assassinating political figures or targeting a civilian population. It has occurred since ancient times. But this book will focus on terrorism in the nineteenth and twentieth centuries as an aid to understanding contemporary terrorism in its most virulent form, as witnessed by all on September 11, 2001.

Terrorism in its modern form developed during the second half of the nineteenth century, often as an outgrowth of utopian anarchist or nationalist movements. The targets of these terrorist acts were government officials or heads of state. In Russia during this period, Vera Zasulich shot St. Petersburg's governor general, Dmitry Trepov (1876); Sophia Perovskaya and Andrei Zhelyabov formed the group responsible for the death of Tsar Alexander II (1881); and Ivan Kalyaev, a Socialist Revolutionary, threw a bomb at the carriage carrying Grand Duke Sergei Aleksandrovich, governor general of Moscow, in 1905. World War I began as a result of the assassination of Austrian Archduke Franz Ferdinand in Sarajevo in 1914. King Alexander I of Yugoslavia and French foreign minister Louis Barthou were both assassinated in 1934 in Marseilles.

Political assassinations continued during the second half of the twentieth century: President John F. Kennedy was assassinated in 1963; Spanish prime minister Admiral Luis Carrero Blanco was killed in 1973 by Basque separatists; Lord Louis Mountbatten by the Irish Republican

Army in 1979; Egyptian president Anwar Sadat by Islamist conspirators; Indian prime minister Indira Ghandi by Sikh separatists in 1984; and Israeli prime minister Yitzhak Rabin by Jewish extremists in 1995. Over time, however, terrorists have moved away from targeting individual leaders in favor of striking at masses of the civilian populace. The release of sarin gas in the Tokyo subway by the Aum Shinrikyo terrorist network in 1995 is one such example.

In the second half of the twentieth century, terrorism took on two further characteristics. First, it became primarily a tool of religious and political groups with separatist or extremist agendas. As such, it was widely used by leftist extremist organizations like the Red Brigades, for example, who used terror tactics against "the powerful of this world" in their quest to overthrow capitalism. Initially, terrorism was largely a national matter. The Basque separatists of Spain (ETA) or Egypt's religious extremists, such as the Muslim Brotherhood, had ties to similar organizations abroad, but their terrorist strikes were largely confined to their own countries. Aum Shinrikyo, though its network spread across many countries, nonetheless carried out its terrorist acts at home in Japan. This has also begun to change. Contemporary terrorism has acquired such a broad international reach that it has become a global concern.

All of these developments can be observed in the rise and development of Russia's own homegrown terrorist movements grouped around Chechen separatists. Chechen terrorist violence was directed toward civilian populations in central and southern Russia—Moscow, St. Petersburg, Budennovsk, Cherkassk, Pervomaisk, Armavir, Vladikavkaz, Mineral'nye Vody, and other cities—and has claimed the lives of several hundred innocent civilians, including children, women, and the elderly. Just as the situation in Chechnya had begun to stabilize—no small achievement—Chechen rebels took their terrorism outside the region and started to strike at those Chechens who actively supported the Russian Federation.

Chechen separatists have extensive ties to terrorist organizations abroad. They have learned by example how to mobilize and distribute extensive terrorist resources through an international network from one country to another: many Chechen field commanders received training at camps in Afghanistan; Arab "volunteers" take part in terrorist acts in

Russia; and Chechen fighters have been, and apparently still are, found in the ranks of al Qaeda, Osama bin Laden's terrorist organization.

The Rise of "Independent" Terrorism

In some cases, international terrorism arose and grew in tandem with particular states and state structures. Iran during the period immediately after the shah's overthrow was typical: the official policy of the nascent Islamic republic was to forcibly export its revolution abroad.

By the end of the twentieth century, however, with the end of the cold war, terrorism had begun to shed its connection to state or government structures. Certain terrorist groups continued to enjoy a degree of state support, but overall this support sharply declined. The decline has largely been the result of policies carried out by the leading international players—Russia, Europe, and the United States—as they emerged from the cold war and began to work together to end state sponsorship of terrorism. The United States relied mainly on political pressure, sanctions, and even the use of force. Russia espoused a more balanced approach consisting primarily of political measures, and many countries, including European Union (EU) member states, have taken the same approach.

Such efforts have borne fruit. Libya, which during the 1980s was considered to be one of the leading state sponsors of terrorism, is no longer providing financial support and training facilities to terrorist groups. As director of the Russian Foreign Intelligence Service (FIS), I was sent to Tripoli to help facilitate this change in Libyan policy. I had fruitful discussions with Libyan leaders, and I know how effective my European colleagues were in this area as well. In the mid- to late 1990s, Muammar Qaddafi broke off relations with the Italian Red Brigades and with the IRA. He expelled the Abu Nidal terrorist organization and severed relations with two extremist Palestinian groups: the Popular Front for the Liberation of Palestine-General Command (PFLP-GC) and the Palestinian Islamic Jihad. Libya also expelled individuals suspected of terrorism and who had worked to overthrow or undermine regimes in Egypt, Yemen, and Jordan.

The United States also played a significant role in Libya's change. In return for Libya's extradition of two Libyan citizens accused in the 1989

Lockerbie Pan Am bombing (which claimed 270 lives, including 189 Americans), the United States agreed to let Libya choose the procedure and venue of the trial. The trial was conducted not in the United States or Great Britain, as the United States had first insisted, but in The Hague at the end of January 2001. In turn, such constructive efforts led Libya to support the U.S. antiterrorist operation in Afghanistan and encouraged Qaddafi to pay compensation to the families of those who perished in the Lockerbie bombing.

During the 1990s several positive changes also took place in Iran. The sympathies of the Iranian people began to shift away from the religious center in Qum and toward Mohammad Khatami, a more moderate spiritual leader known for his restraint. Khatami had spoken out against supporting extremism in society, religion, and foreign policy. He was in favor of reform and freedom of the press. That change had come to Iran was made clear when Khatami won the presidential election by a wide margin and when the 2000 Majlis elections brought reform-minded leaders into the parliamentary majority. Primarily because of the shift in popular opinion, Iran has ceased to use forceful means to spread its religion-based model of state and society to other countries in the region.

Russia and the EU also played a constructive role with respect to Iran by maintaining policies supporting positive domestic development in Iran and reducing Iran's isolation from the rest of the world.

Changes in the attitudes of leading U.S. politicians toward Iran took place during the final years of the Clinton administration. I sensed this during the many discussions I had on Iran with Secretary of State Madeleine Albright. In a March 2000 speech, she underscored the importance of the new positive relations between the United States and Iran and called for an open, clean-slate dialogue between the two countries. At this point the United States' European allies were already engaged in active "critical dialogue" with Iran.

Albright's call was not taken up by the Bush administration. Nevertheless, Bush's policies had sustained a positive note, despite the complexity of Iran's domestic politics. Thus Iran—even though no one seemed to notice—supported the U.S. action in Afghanistan from the very beginning and contributed to U.S. military success in those areas of Afghanistan where it had influence.

Despite these positive trends, the United States became more sharply critical of Iran. Rather abruptly, the Bush administration identified Iran as one of the next possible targets for U.S. antiterrorist action after Afghanistan. This had a counterproductive effect: the moderate and radical-traditionalist factions in Iran began to come closer together. In response to Israeli armed military action in the Palestinian Authority, Hezbollah, supported by Tehran, immediately stepped up its artillery attacks on Israeli-controlled northern Galilee from Lebanon.

But the general trend in the early years of the twenty-first century has been for terrorist groups to become less closely tied to governments. The events of September 11 clearly demonstrated a new, more dangerous kind of international terrorism: criminal acts committed by a self-sufficient group, unaffiliated with any kind of national government, that result in the loss of thousands of innocent lives. This type of terrorist group burst onto the international scene as an entirely new kind of actor.

Until now, the course of international affairs had been dictated by the actions of states—alliances and wars, cooperation and confrontation. In other words, the international climate was a result of the relations between individual states or groups of states and the rise and fall of their alliances. The contemporary international system was defined by state actors and the official international organizations that they created. Now this model is obsolete.

If the organization that had committed this act of terrorism against the United States had been affiliated with any government at all in the Near East, Middle East, Africa, or Southeast Asia, at least one of the leading intelligence agencies in the world—Russia's FIS, the Central Intelligence Agency (CIA), Britain's MI6, Germany's Bundesnachrichtendienst (BND, Federal Intelligence Service), or their counterparts in France, China, India, or another country—would have known about the connection. It is difficult to imagine any Middle Eastern country whose governmental workings are so thoroughly shielded from foreign intelligence services that the latter would have no inside sources of information at all. I cannot imagine that any intelligence service in the world would not have passed on to the Americans information it might have had regarding any potential catastrophic terrorist act on American soil.

I make this statement on the basis of years of personal experience as head of the Russian FIS.

Moreover, the state connection would have been uncovered because it is clear that preparations for the criminal acts committed on September 11 took place over a long period. According to David Sedney, deputy chief of mission at the U.S. embassy in Kabul, the terrorists began to gather forces in the United States two years earlier. They began to build up financial resources, and the individual hijackers trained to pilot commercial passenger aircraft. Not just anyone is granted access to such training, and not just anyone is competent to complete it. If nothing else, falsified documentation had to be created that would not raise suspicions—a specialized and painstaking process. Individuals with good documentation were able to travel freely and unnoticed from country to country.

The support of many individuals was required to plan and execute this operation. Several airline terminals were infiltrated, and baggage security checkpoints were breached. At least four airliners were simultaneously hijacked with their passengers; additional hijackings may have been planned. The hijackers evaded radar tracking and made synchronized strikes against predetermined targets. This entire effort took place with no appreciable leak of information. A criminal organization of this magnitude must certainly be quite powerful, well networked, financially secure, and autonomous.

The FBI and other U.S. intelligence agencies are investigating alleged members of this organization, which the United States determined to be led by Osama bin Laden, a Saudi multimillionaire who was living in Afghanistan under the protection of the Taliban regime. The United States will almost certainly make public some information learned from the investigation, including details obtained by questioning members of bin Laden's al Qaeda terrorist group. After their arrest during the U.S. military operation in Afghanistan, suspected al Qaeda members were held in isolation at the U.S. naval base at Guantanamo Bay in Cuba. I trust that information obtained from these individuals will not be used to create a trumped-up case against any "rogue" state, but will instead corroborate the autonomous nature of this criminal organization.

The intelligence community was hit with an avalanche of criticism in connection with the September 11 terrorist attacks. That the U.S. intelligence agencies bore the brunt of this seems wrong to me. The infiltration of an organization as isolated, as self-contained, and as highly disciplined as al Qaeda is an extremely difficult feat.

Yet U.S. intelligence agencies did undoubtedly have a general idea about bin Laden and his activities. Testifying before the Senate Armed Services Committee on February 2, 1999, CIA director George Tenet stated: "There is not the slightest doubt that Osama bin Laden, his worldwide allies, and his sympathizers are planning further attacks against us. ... Bin Laden's organization has contacts virtually worldwide, including in the United States—and he has stated unequivocally, Mr. Chairman, that all Americans are targets." Naturally, with information of this nature, the CIA and the FBI should have conducted a thorough investigation of bin Laden's organization.

This effort had to have taken place. The American press reported—and National Security Advisor Condoleezza Rice confirmed—that on August 6, one month before the tragedy, President Bush was given a CIA report mentioning that bin Laden's people were planning some type of attack on the United States using airplanes. But the report contained no specific information and therefore was not accorded the attention it perhaps should have received. Angered by charges of incompetence, U.S. intelligence made another leak to the press: that in July 2001, an FBI agent in Arizona reported that potential hijackers might be training at U.S. flight schools, and that this information had been passed to those in authority. At the time, this information was disregarded as well. I do not believe that the CIA or the FBI provided incomplete information out of fear for their informants. Most likely they simply had no detailed information.

This example should serve as a warning to the global intelligence community. Obviously, today's new circumstances dictate that we step up cooperative investigation of certain countries and that we increase information sharing, including establishing a collective database of terrorist organizations and their members. But even this is not enough. Joint efforts in areas of *mutual interest*—the war against terrorism is one such area, certainly—must include collective analysis and interpretation of information gathered. We must seek and establish ways to carry out this cooperative analysis. This is one of the lessons learned from September 11.

When I was head of Russia's FIS (1991–95), we did have some success establishing contacts with the NATO intelligence community.[1] During the cold war this would have been unthinkable, but in the early to mid-1990s, these contacts were beneficial to all. Now a new stage has been reached. In areas as sensitive to us all as terrorism, perhaps it is time to conduct joint operations. Obviously, few intelligence services will be willing to reveal their sources. This should not be allowed to hinder the creation of a shared database, the swift analysis of sensitive information, or the possibility of joint or parallel coordinated operations.

None of this in any way diminishes the importance of national intelligence services. National intelligence agencies will continue to operate, but they should steer away from methods universally deemed no longer appropriate for today's world.

Osama bin Laden

The course of Osama bin Laden's life and the development of his terrorist network have been shaped by many trends and events in the second half of the twentieth century. After the collapse of colonialism, the center of radicalism in the Muslim world shifted from the anticolonial liberation movements to militant Islam. During the cold war the United States and the Soviet Union attracted to themselves, sometimes recklessly, as many different movements and organizations as possible. The Soviet invasion of Afghanistan created conditions that brought the United States closer to some of the most reactionary Muslim groups. Sometimes, these groups coalesced and began operation as a result of direct American involvement. The Soviet withdrawal from Afghanistan and the end of the cold war changed this situation. Radical, militant Muslim groups began to change their orientation and came to see the United States as their primary adversary. The vacuum that developed in the immediate post–cold war period, with the ending of institutionalized, global competition between the superpowers, allowed militant Islamists to build their power base.

Osama bin Laden was born on June 28, 1957, in Saudi Arabia, one of more than fifty children fathered by an extremely successful business-man, Mohammed Awad bin Laden, who founded the Saudi bin Laden Group in 1931. This company gradually grew and diversified, becoming powerful in the oil and chemical industries, in banking, in telecommu-nications, and in satellite communications. As of 2000, the Group com-prised some sixty affiliate and daughter companies in Asia, Europe, and the United States.

In January 2003, while participating in an international economic forum in Jeddah, I was invited to tour the headquarters of this company, one of Saudi Arabia's most powerful and influential. My colleagues and I were warmly received and taken around by the company's president—Osama bin Laden's brother. When I asked if he was still in contact with Osama, he answered categorically that he was not, adding, "Every family has its bad apple."

Be that as it may, the only son of Mohammed's tenth wife, Osama bin Laden inherited $250 million upon his father's death in addition to receiving—in accordance with strict Saudi custom—a portion of his family's construction interests. In twenty years he was able to double or triple this fortune. Thus Osama bin Laden had the means and where-withal to create and launch entire organizations without any need for state sponsorship.

Oddly enough, American intelligence participated in establishing bin Laden and his organization. There is reason to believe that the United States first approached bin Laden after he had finished his studies in eco-nomics and management at King Abdul Aziz University in Jeddah, when he devoted himself to the cause of jihad against the Soviets in Afghanistan. Bin Laden attracted attention because he created the Mak-tab al-Khidamat (MAK or Services Office), the precursor to al Qaeda, which maintained centers in various countries, including two in the United States (in Detroit and Brooklyn), to recruit soldiers to fight against the Soviets in Afghanistan. The MAK recruited and sent to Afghanistan thousands of mercenaries, and it organized training camps there and in Pakistan. In organizing action against the Soviets, bin Laden cooperated closely with the CIA's Cyclone operation, which contributed as much as $500 million a year to Afghan rebels. According to some sources, it was bin Laden's idea to arm the Afghani mujahidin with Stinger missiles. The United States had begun to deliver the missiles to Afghanistan, where they were used against Soviet aircraft and helicopters.

In general during the cold war, most military operations launched or supported in third countries to counter the Americans or the Soviets were unstable. Such groups often broke free from their initial sponsors and sometimes even turned against them. Even in regional conflicts, this same rule held fast. After all, Hamas was originally created by the Mossad, the Israeli secret service, to weaken the Palestine Liberation Organization (PLO) in the occupied West Bank. Over time, however, the Israelis lost control of this group.

The same occurred with the al Qaeda group formed by bin Laden in 1987 on the basis of the MAK. At first, its actions were limited to within Afghanistan. But after the Soviet withdrawal that same year, al Qaeda became highly anti-American and began to attract not just Arabs, but Sunni Muslims in general. In February 1998, al Qaeda publicly called on all Muslims everywhere to kill American citizens—both military and civilian—and those who supported them.

Al Qaeda quickly gained terrorist experience. Its range has extended to Yemen, Somalia, and the United States. In August 1998 two bombs exploded simultaneously at U.S. embassies in Nairobi, Kenya, and Dar-es-Salaam, Tanzania, killing more than two hundred people and wounding approximately four thousand. Bin Laden openly applauded these acts but in neither case claimed that al Qaeda was responsible. In this respect, bin Laden and his group differ from other terrorists, who immediately claim responsibility for such acts to demonstrate to the world how powerful they are. Apparently, al Qaeda's self-sufficiency and financial independence make it possible for the group to keep a low profile.

This also enables al Qaeda to avoid dependence on state sponsors. Much has been written, for example, about the ties of bin Laden and al Qaeda to Saudi Arabia. Bin Laden coordinated operations from Riyadh while the Soviets were in Afghanistan, but after he turned against the United States, his interests and those of the Saudis coincided very little. Anxious about U.S. reaction, the Saudis deported bin Laden (he had returned there after the Soviets left Afghanistan) and subsequently stripped him of Saudi citizenship. Bin Laden was also forced to leave

Sudan, where he had gone from Saudi Arabia: Khartoum did not want any problems on his account either.

Apparently, bin Laden did not have ties with Iraq either. After Iraq's invasion of Kuwait, bin Laden offered the Saudi leadership to send thousands of his soldiers to fight against Saddam Hussein. These soldiers had been "unemployed" since the Soviet troops left Afghanistan.

Neither would Iran have become a partner to bin Laden, since the al Qaeda leader supported the Sunni Taliban in their fight against the primarily Shiite Northern Alliance in Afgahnistan. Shiite Iran was fighting against the Taliban.

The Taliban was the only group with which bin Laden was on good terms. But the Taliban was more of a movement than anything approaching a governmental regime, and he had to work to establish a relationship even with it. Bin Laden had given his eldest daughter in marriage to Mullah Mohammed Omar, the Taliban leader, and had publicly given other signs of being close to the Taliban. In reality, however, he controlled his own operations and facilities in Afghanistan—he was a completely autonomous entity who remained in his fortified system of caves and underground tunnels—dug during the Soviet war—right up until the United States began its military action in Afghanistan. Bin Laden and the Taliban also shared in an illegal drug trade that increased al Qaeda's financial resources, and bin Laden helped launder Taliban money using, among others, the Chechen mafia, where there were also complications. After 1998, American intelligence services were in active contact with the Taliban on issues related to the cessation of their drug trafficking. At the same time, al Qaeda was expanding its drug business.

The fact that al Qaeda had not been assimilated into the Taliban movement and, moreover, that there were Talibs who opposed it, was borne out by Mullah Mohammed Khaksar, a former Taliban intelligence chief.[2] According to Khaksar, he even offered to help the United States remove the Taliban leader, Mullah Mohammed Omar, in 1999 because he "believed that under Mullah Omar the Taliban had become a puppet, first of Pakistani intelligence and then of Osama bin Laden and his al Qaeda." Khaksar said the offer was made in Peshawar to U.S. diplomats Gregory Marchese and J. Peter McIllwain. No response was received.

It would not be out of place to point out that the Taliban extremist Islamic movement, which seized power in Kabul to control the entire country, was also formed with help from the United States. As Russian foreign minister, I met with Pakistan's former prime minister Benazir Bhutto, who made no secret of the fact that the Taliban were brought into existence by Pakistani military intelligence with the help of the American CIA. So it is possible that Khaksar's acquaintance with American diplomats had been a long one.

Regardless of the details, it is clear that the Taliban openly welcomed bin Laden and his al Qaeda network to Afghanistan, primarily because they shared the same ideology: adherence to the ideas of radical, militant Islam. Al Qaeda's autonomy did not hinder but, rather, helped expand the organization's sphere of influence. In taking up the flag of militant Islam, bin Laden proclaimed his goal to be the establishment of a "true Islamic state that rules according to *sharia* and unites all Muslims throughout the world." According to his *bayan*—the proclamations he periodically makes—Islam is not practiced by separate groups of people. There is a single Muslim nation. Bin Laden uses these principles to rationalize his aid to extremists in Algeria and Egypt and his financial support of Palestinian terrorist groups.

Current evidence indicates that bin Laden lent substantial support to Albanian separatists in Kosovo, in particular to the anti-Serbian Kosovo Liberation Army, which the U.S. State Department first correctly identified as terrorists but which they later supported for geopolitical reasons. The ideological underpinning of this support was bin Laden's goal to create an extremist Islamic state in the center of Europe, comprising Albania, Kosovo, the Sanjak, and parts of Bosnia, Macedonia, and Montenegro. The fact that the Balkans were a major route for moving drugs from Afghanistan into western Europe was also of major significance to bin Laden.

In the latter half of the 1990s, a highly developed terrorist infrastructure came into being in Afghanistan, made up of training camps and command posts that directed militant groups in Egypt, Algeria, India, Saudi Arabia, Tajikistan, and several other countries. The network had satellite communications, a printing operation, and large caches of modern weapons and ammunition. Moreover, this movement was drawing recruits from all over the Muslim world. Yossef Bodansky, an American expert on international terrorism, wrote, "In the Badr 1 and Badr 2 camps . . . more and more volunteers are showing up from Central Asia and the Caucasus."[3]

There is also much evidence connecting bin Laden and al Qaeda with Chechen rebels. Both Arab and non-Arab members of these groups underwent training in Afghanistan. It was there that bin Laden, according to some, met the Jordanian Omar Ibn al Khattab, who later became one of Chechnya's most powerful warlords. Khattab later introduced bin Laden to another Chechen separatist leader, Shamil Basaev.

A Terrifying Prospect

So, there is convincing evidence that autonomous, self-sufficient organizations are at work in the global arena, and that they advocate mass terror as a means of achieving their goals. We have focused until now on only one of them: al Qaeda. But there is no guarantee that al Qaeda is unique. Moreover, such organizations are low-profile and tend not to take credit for the terrorist acts they commit. Rather, the large scale of their terrorist acts and the number of victims they claim are most important to them.

When the only players in international politics were nation-states, trends and events were significantly more predictable and thus more easily controlled. After World War II, the United States and the USSR headed opposing ideological systems, and each possessed a nuclear arsenal that could destroy the other. They kept each other in check. States that attached themselves to one or the other of these ideological systems found themselves under the control of the superpowers. Those who were not part of this system also behaved with restraint, taking extra care to make sure that their conflicts did not expand outside regional boundaries. During this period, terrorism did not pose a serious *international* threat.

And now, in this changed world? How can even the most militarily powerful nations ensure the safety and security of their citizens?

The situation is complicated by the fact that nuclear weapons and other weapons of mass destruction (WMD)—chemical, biological, and radiological—are hardly inaccessible to these autonomous terrorist groups. Bin Laden's al Qaeda is but one of a long list of terrorist organizations. According to CIA director George Tenet, "Bin Laden's organization is just one of about a dozen terrorist groups that have expressed an interest in or have sought chemical, biological, radiological, and nuclear (CBRN) agents. Bin Laden, for example, has called the acquisition of these weapons a 'religious duty' and noted that 'how we use them is up to us.'"

As we enter the twenty-first century, the world is ever more vulnerable to the use of WMD in cultivating terror. First, nonallegiance to any government body allows terrorist organizations to sail into "uncharted waters" with incredible freedom to maneuver. Second, the ability of terrorists to finance themselves has grown. Third, the spread of terror using WMD is greatly aided by the process of globalization, which has made information freely available and removed countless barriers and limitations that previously existed. Last, technological developments have made smaller and much more compact nuclear devices possible and are making it easier to produce chemical and biological weapons. All these factors make weapons of mass destruction much more accessible to terrorists.

Does bin Laden's organization already possess weapons of mass destruction? The U.S. State Department's official list of charges against Osama bin Laden states that al Qaeda has tried to acquire nuclear weapons or their components since 1993. During the U.S. military action in Afghanistan, U.S. intelligence agents found technical documentation for nuclear warheads in an al Qaeda building in Kabul. They also uncovered evidence that two Pakistani physicists had been in Afghanistan during the Taliban's rule.

There is reason to believe that al Qaeda has come very close to possessing radiological weapons. U.S. attorney general John Ashcroft stated that Abdullah al-Muhajir (also known as Jose Padilla) was on an al Qaeda reconnaissance mission for a planned attack on Washington using a radioactive dirty bomb. Arrested on May 8, 2002, after flying into Chicago's O'Hare airport from Pakistan, al-Muhajir also allegedly planned to release toxic substances in large U.S. hotels.[4] Based on the interrogation of Abu Zubaydah, a top al Qaeda leader captured in Pakistan, U.S. defense secretary Donald Rumsfeld told reporters in April 2002 that the network was trying to build a radiological bomb.

By all accounts, it would seem the world is now quite close to seeing the use of some kind of nuclear device by terrorists. And there are hundreds of targets in every large country that possesses nuclear material: nuclear weapons stockpiles or transport caravans, nuclear power stations, nuclear fuel laboratories. The destruction of any of these would be a nuclear disaster of catastrophic proportions. At the beginning of 2002, forty-three nations had nuclear power stations or nuclear reactors capable of producing nuclear material. More than one hundred nations are stockpiling reserves of radioactive material. There is no convincing reason to believe that all this nuclear material is well managed or protected.

Finally, international terrorism is particularly dangerous in light of the spread of nuclear weapons to more and more nations that are involved in regional conflicts. When the United States began its action in Afghanistan, for example, a strong movement supporting the Taliban rose up in neighboring Pakistan. Hundreds of thousands of Pakistanis marched in Islamabad, Karachi, and other cities demanding that the "pro-American" government be ousted.

At the same time, the Pakistani government saw fit to remove several highly placed but unreliable officers from duty. I think many justifiably feared that an overthrow of the Pakistani government by pro-Taliban groups—which include some in the Pakistani army—would give the Taliban access to nuclear weapons. In this case it was a false alarm. But what about the next time?

As Russian foreign minister, I met President Bill Clinton in September 1996 in New York. Speaking about the great importance of cooperation between Russia and the United States, the president identified the most critical political problem for the next twenty-five years as the Indian-Pakistani conflict and the threat that it would progress toward the use of nuclear weapons. I admit I was somewhat surprised by his choice; I do not think that possession of nuclear weapons by both those nations necessarily means the weapons will be used in a conflict. Both sides also honestly hope to avoid a tragedy of this magnitude through careful and deliberate diplomacy in their conflict and through broad international efforts. But it would be another matter entirely if nuclear weapons were to fall into the hands of an independent terrorist organization.

In the war on international terrorism, it is extremely important to take decisive and direct action supporting the nonproliferation of WMD. Despite valuable progress—in particular the signing of the Nuclear Non-Proliferation Treaty (NPT) by the majority of the world's nations—the global community remains passive. It is far from clear what specific action can be taken to block nations, especially those engaged in regional conflicts, from joining the nuclear club. But the September 11 tragedy demands that we give the issue our full attention. I see this as one of the primary tasks for Russian diplomacy and Russian special services—especially since the two undeclared nuclear nations and many of the threshold nuclear nations lie at Russia's door.

While Russian-American relations have entered a new phase of greater mutual trust, the United States must cease unjustifiably accusing us of poorly managing our nuclear material and of working with other countries to build nuclear power plants that are supposedly used to produce nuclear weapons. Instead of such rhetoric—which does little to stop the spread of nuclear weapons—we would like to see close cooperation toward the antiterrorism objectives we share.

Each time I met with Strobe Talbott, Madeleine Albright, or Al Gore as head of the Russian government, or, before that, as foreign minister, they would invariably rake me over the coals for our nuclear power plant construction in Bushehr, Iran. They would present me with the same list of Russian firms and companies that were supposedly supplying Iran with technology that could be used to produce nuclear weapons. We knew about their list because it had been given to us earlier by the Israeli government. We would explain that the construction in Bushehr was being carried out under the strict oversight of the International Atomic Energy Agency (IAEA); that many of the companies on their list were no longer to be found at the addresses they showed; that we were delivering the same kind of light water reactors that the United States was getting ready to give North Korea; or that for Iran to have nuclear weapons was clearly not in Russia's interest—first and foremost for purely geographical reasons.

Today, of course, demarches like these should be a thing of the past. Just like any other nation, Russia bears sole responsibility for any violations of international obligations currently in force. Our simple rule of thumb is that there should be no such violations.

The multitude of existing documents—UN Security Council resolutions and various conventions and declarations adopted by the UN General Assembly and its special bodies, by the Council of Europe, by the Organization of American States, by the League of Arab States, by many national parliaments, and by a number of international conferences—falls short. We must develop a comprehensive document, a charter, for the war on terrorism. One prominent expert on international law, G. I. Morozov, correctly asserts that terrorism must not be viewed as a political crime. It is by its very nature a criminal act. Morozov insists that national laws on statutes of limitations, or on the right of nonextradition, do not apply to terrorist crimes.[5] Any charter on terrorism must make issues like this clear.

That such a charter will sooner or later be signed seems a certainty. We do not need to specify exact contents—a task requiring international consultation and negotiation—to be able to anticipate several of the measures it would provide for.

Nations that sign the charter would make a binding agreement not to permit within their borders any group or organization that advocates terrorism to achieve its goals, regardless of how noble or desirable those goals might seem. Any signatory to the charter would undertake strict financial oversight of terrorist groups, as well as measures to prohibit the transport of weapons, ammunition, or troops by them. The charter could include any number of additional requirements or provisions for nations who agree to take an uncompromising line against terrorism.

I would like to emphasize that it is the responsibility of all states that sign the charter to turn over terrorists that seek a haven within their borders, at the request of any other signatory and with sufficient and appropriate documented evidence. Extradition of accused terrorists is essential in the war on terrorism: criminals should not be able to count on shelter from any state. No matter where they are, they should find no quarter. At present there are many states that do not share extradition agreements, a situation that often interferes with efforts to bring criminals to justice.

Changing extradition laws and legislation on a national level is a long and arduous process. These obstacles would melt away with a charter on terrorism.

The global community must agree to reevaluate many previously accepted beliefs about ensuring nations' own security and that of their allies. They must take part in establishing and maintaining regional and global stability. Essential to this is that we find reliable means of combating international terrorism in all its new forms. The war on terrorism will not be effective unless all forces for good in the world join together in this common goal—and this includes the world's one billion Muslims.

2

THE AGGRESSION OF ISLAM: TRUTH OR FICTION?

Immediately following the September 11 attacks, a wave of anti-Islamic sentiment rolled across the United States and western Europe. President Bush was quick to publicly visit a mosque, and British prime minister Tony Blair published several articles in Muslim newspapers in Great Britain, but these actions had no significant effect on reducing tension. Isolated efforts such as these, however well-intentioned, were not enough to change public reaction. Moreover, the September 11 attacks were immediately followed by articles in the press in the United States and Europe characterizing Islam as aggressive and warlike by nature and noting, even more alarmingly, that aggression was on the rise within the Islamic world.

The events of September 11 focused much attention on a thesis put forth by Harvard professor Samuel Huntington. He argued that the old bipolar cold war model of international relations is being replaced by a model based on unavoidable competition between civilizations. Huntington divides the world into western and nonwestern civilizations (such as Confucian, Islamic, and Hindu). Western democracy, he warns, will find itself face to face with the extremism and fundamentalism of other civilizations and must prepare for an epic showdown. Huntington overlooks economic or political roots of conflict, seeing cultural and religious issues at the heart of the matter. Understandably, this paradigm ushers in a new post–cold war division of the world along cultural and religious rather than ideological lines.[1]

The false equation of international terrorism with Islam, and of a few extremist Muslim minorities with the Muslim world as a whole, forces the world closer to such a division. The course of the twenty-first century depends largely on whether or not this trend can be stopped.

The Muslim world is not an entity unto itself. There are six million Muslims in the United States, where Islam is the fastest growing religion. Millions of Muslims have immigrated to Europe from Turkey, Albania, North Africa, Syria, Lebanon, Pakistan, India, Indonesia, Malaysia, and the Philippines, and their numbers are not declining. In many places, they are beginning to form geographically identifiable communities. Muslims have long been a part of Russia as well. Many of the areas in Russia with dense Muslim populations were territories that historically joined with or were annexed by Russia. Approximately twenty million Muslims live in Russia today.

Obviously, a cultural-religious division of the world would constitute a serious threat to Russian federalism. The contours of such a division stretch not only across the globe but through the very heart of many nations as well. Even the slightest move toward division along these lines fosters the increase of separatism, which is one of the most dangerous threats to international security in the contemporary world. The specter of separatism already threatens a significant number of countries today. Still others may be threatened with separatism in the future if things take a bad turn. No one nation, even the most harmonious of multinational countries in the world today, is immune to this threat.

The right of separation is an integral part of one of democracy's cherished principles, the right of self-determination. Separation was a useful right for people struggling to free themselves from colonial rule. The principle of self-determination up to and including separation was broadly accepted and figures prominently in the Charter of the United Nations.

This formula, however, is outdated. Many new sovereign nations emerged after the collapse of colonialism in the 1960s. And new nations emerged in place of the former Soviet Union, Czechoslovakia, and Yugoslavia in the 1990s. One of the primary goals of the international community for the foreseeable future is stabilization, both within nations and on an international level. An essential factor in this effort is reaffirmation of the principle of a nation's territorial integrity. Any different conclusion will set in motion a chain of events that will cover the globe with countless hotbeds of violence. If any national or ethnic group is given the right to secede or form an independent nation-state at will, international relations will be plunged into chaos. There are already examples where this issue has come to the forefront. Attempts to defend Albanian separatists in Kosovo had the unintended result of Albanians' trying to separate Kosovo from Yugoslavia while systematically driving the Serbs out. Global democracy cannot be used to justify the spread of separatism. In the case of Kosovo, Albanian separatism could lead to the outbreak of large-scale warfare throughout the Balkans, and perhaps even extending beyond.

This is precisely the threat that exists in Chechnya and its surrounding territory.

Rejecting the idea that national or ethnic groups have an inherent right to separation and self-government in no way diminishes the nationality problem or the need to find solutions to it. But the right to self-determination should not trump the preservation of a nation's territorial integrity. Accordingly, the creation of new nations is not possible on the basis of a unilateral decision of a given national or ethnic group to separate, but only on the agreement of the populations in both parts of the country: the part that wants to separate and the part that remains.

If such an agreement is not in fact reached, then the logical resolution is internal autonomy that preserves the unity of the original state. The autonomy granted to the self-determining national or ethnic group should provide the broadest possible economic, political, and cultural rights.

Global division along cultural-religious lines would have an extremely destabilizing effect, both internationally and within sovereign states. Accordingly, world civilization should work toward absorbing and reflecting all the best and brightest features of today's cultural diversity.

The Roots of Terrorism Are Not in the Quran

It is a fact that Islam—like Christianity, Judaism, or Buddhism—is a product of its culture and has an enormous influence on the development of the civilizations where it is prevalent.[2] However, history has proven that civilizations—and their greatest single feature, religion—are nothing if not interdependent and that their development is nothing if not intertwined. The Old Testament is a holy book for both Jews and Christians. The Quran incorporates much from both these world religions. Muslims believe the Quran to be God's revelation to the people through His chosen prophet, Muhammad (who thus was closer than anyone else to the true word of God). The Quran does not contradict Jewish or Christian prophets. However, in many instances the "truth" of those books is overridden by later, more recent revelations of the Lord in the Quran. For example, the Quran[3] accuses Jewish holy men of distorting the Torah, which says (according to Muslim interpretation) that a new prophet shall be sent to Arabia (2:79).

In the first translations of the Quran, "Allah" was usually translated as "God." Now, the word Allah is usually left untranslated, which might create the impression that Muslims believe in a different god. Yet the Quran states, "And do not dispute with the followers of the Book except by what is best, except those of them who act unjustly, and say: We believe in that which has been revealed to us and revealed to you, and our God and your God is One, and to Him do we submit" (29:46).

Muslim scholars made enormous contributions to science, art, and learning. In 980, Ibn Sina (Avicenna) published *al-Qanun fi'l-tibb* (Canon on Medicine), which remained the greatest and best-known work on medicine in Europe until the seventeenth century. Muslim philosophers greatly influenced the theologian Thomas Aquinas (1226–74). The works of Aristotle survived only through their translation into Arabic by Muslim scholars. Ibn Khaldun (1332–1406) is rightly called the greatest historian of the Middle Ages. Jabir ibn Haiyan, the alchemist Geber of the Middle Ages, is generally known as the father of chemistry, and the very word chemistry comes from the Arabic *al-kimia*. The word algorithm reflects the name of Muslim mathematician al-Khowarizmi, who first described the concept of algorithms and whose writings were used as textbooks in the universities of Europe until the sixteenth century. The examples go on and on.

Without question, western civilization also greatly influenced the Islamic world.

Has the mechanism of intercultural influence ceased? No, of course not. Indeed, increasing globalization cannot help but result in the world's diverse cultures' affecting one another as they move closer together in the bosom of a global civilization. This is the way things are headed. But this evolution could be hampered if the world is induced to divide along religious lines.

In striving to force absolute adherence to their ideas on the entire Muslim world, Islamic extremists use the Quran—or rather, a dogmatic, one-sided interpretation of it—to justify their actions. Isolated phrases plucked from the verses of the Quran should hardly be taken as representative of the religion as a whole. In fact, while some phrases may be construed as calls to violence, many others call for peace and tolerance.

In this connection, there are two important tenets from the Quran and from the "Principles of Islamic Law Concerning the War against Infidels," compiled in the Middle Ages by the Muslim scholar al-Quduri. First: in the use of force against enemies of Islam, Muslims are instructed not to cause harm to civilians—to women, children, or the elderly. It is stated in the "Principles" that Muslims "should not commit treachery or deviate from the right path. You must not mutilate dead bodies. Neither kill a child, nor a woman, nor an aged man. Or the infirm, the blind, or the handicapped, if they do not participate in war with their counsel, or unless the woman is a queen. It is not permissible to kill the mentally ill."[4]

"And fight in the way of Allah with those who fight with you, and do not exceed the limits, surely Allah does not love those who exceed the limits (2:190)." This saying testifies to the defensive nature of those armed actions that might be carried out in the name of the Quran.

The second relevant tenet of the Quran is the prohibition on suicide for Muslims. The recognition of both these tenets is very important, given attempts to equate terrorism with Islam.

The extremely swift and generally peaceful spread of Islam is unique. Triumphant expansion of the Arab world occurred primarily after the death of Muhammad in 632. Under Khalif Omar (634–44), Islam spread to Mesopotamia, Syria, Palestine, and the Caucasus, and into Iran, Egypt, and Cyrenaica (modern-day Libya). In less than fifty years, Islam had reached the borders of China, the Indus River valley, the Atlantic shore, and the Nile rapids. Military conquests were made against Byzantium and Sassanid Iran.

As a rule, Islam was not forced on conquered peoples. According to Islamic scholar Henri Massé, "The ground was often prepared by internal dissensions. We have seen the Arabs welcomed by the Egyptian Copts and by the Syrians almost as saviors. Similarly, in Persia and in Spain the existing governments had already alienated their subjects by misrule. Nevertheless the Arabs softened rather than abolished these troublesome administrations."[5] Massé further asserts that "the conquered peoples embraced Islam not from conviction but in order to pay the lesser tax."[6] Prominent Soviet orientalist Evgeny Belyaev agrees that the "Arabs offered a much more palatable existence to those who yielded to their governance. As a result, most inhabitants of lands conquered by the Arabs offered no resistance, and indeed often acted as allies."[7] Even today, these factors persist. In India, for example, many members of the untouchable caste embrace Islam as a way to escape the social and cultural restrictions they would otherwise endure.

The idea that Islam was adopted part and parcel by subjugated peoples is a false one. The adoption of Islam in Egypt took four centuries, and a significant population of Christian Copts survive there today. Relative tolerance toward nonbelievers not in theory (jihad means holy war against nonbelievers) but in practice is evidenced by the fact that Lebanon is home to the Maronite community (long associated with the country's political system, where its members hold many leading posts— president, commander-in-chief), to Orthodox Christians, and to Christian groups of other denominations.

Even today, Christians constitute a religious minority in many Arab nations. Until the middle of the twentieth century (before immigration to Israel was common), the same could be said of Jewish populations in these countries. Even under conditions characterized by conflict, restrictions, and occasionally persecution, Jews continued to live in Arab nations from generation to generation. And in this respect, it was no worse and no better to live under Islam than in tsarist Russia or in medieval Europe.

The history of Islam has generally been less bloody than that of, say, Catholicism. Islam had nothing resembling the burning of heretics at the stake. The history of Islam contains its bloody moments, but violence had its roots more often than not in ethnic conflict. Only rarely were atrocities committed against those of other faiths, including those the Quran calls "people of the Book" (the Bible)—meaning Jews and Christians. Violence was used in the name of Islam primarily against Muslims who followed different schools. Particularly strong animosity has existed between Sunni and Shiite Muslims, for instance.

When Muhammad began his fight against those in Mecca who had left him and the local Jewish tribes who supported them, and against the Christian tribes of Syria who had joined with Jews to attack him, he exhorted his soldiers to fight bravely, but humanely. Civilians were to be spared. Not one tree was to be toppled, not one house to be destroyed.

True, the prophet showed this restraint primarily during his time in Mecca. His quarrel with the Jews started later and led to the exile of three Jewish tribes from Arabia. But there is no historical record of any bloody pogroms.

Beginning in the eleventh century, Crusaders made attempts to liberate Jerusalem and to retake the nearby Holy Lands from the Muslims by fire and sword. When Jerusalem— the city where Muslims, Jews, and Christians had previously lived peaceably under Muslim rule—fell during the First Crusade, 40,000 Muslims were killed in two days. This historical fact is not an indictment of Christianity as a barbarous or terroristic religion. Orthodox or Eastern Christians at the time managed to live side by side with Muslims, despite occasional conflicts.

These observations—again, based on historical fact—are not made to disparage the extremist ideas widely held among some Muslims, especially in those areas heavily involved in the Arab-Israeli conflict. Such views have their place, and it is unreasonable, if not impossible, to refute them. But these ideas are rooted less in religion than they are in politics. Disagreement with Israel's right to exist was a reaction to the eviction of Palestinians from territory they had settled. It has no basis in the Quran, which teaches not only about Muhammad, prophet of "the one true God, Allah," but mentions other "lesser" prophets: Isa and Musa (Jesus and Moses).

Extremist Arab views on Israel, which run counter to the overwhelming opinion of the rest of the world, have clearly evolved over time. None other than Abdallah, the crown prince of Saudi Arabia, site of the two holiest Muslim shrines, proposed the following in 2002: that Arabs would indeed recognize Israel when it relinquishes the territories it occupied in 1967 during the Six-Day War. One must imagine that this proposal was made not only to bring peace to the Middle East, but also to be more in step with the rest of humanity.

The Difference between Fundamentalism and Extremism

To understand Muslims and their interaction with the rest of the world it is essential to differentiate between Islamic fundamentalism and Islamic extremism. Like any other religious fundamentalism, Islamic fundamentalism endorses religious education and the strict observance of religious traditions in everyday life. The goal of Islamic extremists is to use force to impose what they consider an Islamic government model on state and society and to enforce Islamic rules of behavior in public and private life by violent means.

Extremism has emerged from within Islam not because the religion itself gave rise to it, but as a result of the rise of several Islamic sects, some of which espouse values that are far from the mainstream. An example of such a sect is Wahhabism, whose beliefs are the justification for the illegal activities of many extremists, especially in the Northern Caucasus.

The Wahhabi movement arose in Arabia in the eighteeth century. Its founder, Abd al-Wahhab (1703–92), called for reestablishing the original orthodox Islamic faith. Al-Wahhab spoke out harshly against the spreading cult of Muslim saints, which he saw as a return to polytheism. Based strictly on the Quran and Sunnah, Wahhabism rejected any interpretation of these sources, seeing in this also a slide toward polytheism. These motives led to the renunciation of many values that were an established part of Islam, even the cult of the prophet, who should not be seen as an intercessor, since that would have diminished the greatness of Allah. Wahhabites believed that nothing man-made, not even a prophet's grave, should be revered. They rejected paying homage to the Qaaba in Mecca—the holiest Muslim shrine. And they did not allow oaths or vows in the name of the prophet or his descendants, and they dealt harshly with anyone caught using alcohol, smoking, listening to music, or playing any games at all. Wahhabites characteristically persecuted wealthy Muslims and called for a return to an unspoiled, puritanical form of Islam.

In approximately 1770 a Wahhabi state was established in Nejd (Arabia). During the early nineteenth century, Wahhabites looted Shiite sanctuaries, raiding and sacking Karbala, the Shiite holy city in southern Iraq, and eventually seized control of Mecca in 1803, destroying mosques and vandalizing the Qaaba. After seizing Medina, the Wahhabites defiled Muhammad's grave.

The Wahhabites were stopped in 1818, defeated by the Egyptian ruler Muhammad Ali on orders from the Ottoman government. But they soon reestablished themselves. Having shed many of its more puritanical and radical characteristics, Wahhabism is today the official religion of Saudi Arabia, whose rulers have become fabulously wealthy from oil.

Do the home-grown followers of Wahhabism today in Chechnya and Dagestan fully understand the movement's history and significance?

Throughout history, extremist Islamic ideas have been condemned because they were anachronistic for the age in which they were expressed. Extremist Islam is out of step with the rest of the world and cannot match the historical progress the rest of the world community has made. It is no accident that the leader of the Palestinian people is the Palestine Liberation Organization and not the Palestinian Islamic Jihad. Fifty years ago, in their struggle against King Farouk—whose regime had become corrupt—the Egyptians chose not to follow the extremist religious Muslim Brotherhood, but instead to take up with the Free Officers, led by Gamal Abdel Nasser. After victory in 1953, Nasser capitalized on the benevolent neutrality of the people to harshly put down the Muslim Brotherhood and prevent them from seizing power. Similar scenarios have played out in Algeria and other countries.

Modern-day Islamic extremism focuses less on jihad than on fighting the governments of Muslim countries that chose to follow a secular model to build their nations. This was demonstrated in 1982 in Hama, Syria, when the Muslim Brotherhood attempted a coup under the green flag of Islam. President Hafiz al-Assad ruthlessly crushed the revolt, executing many thousands of the Islamist insurgents.

Extremist forces with designs on power in various Muslim countries have not enjoyed popular support. Muslim society is becoming more and more modernized all the time. These processes are at work even in Saudi Arabia, the birthplace of Islam, where the present generation of Muslims is more politically and socially active than previous generations. People are speaking out in favor of democracy, pluralism, and freedom of expression. Without a doubt, globalization strengthens the democratization of Islam. The Internet alone is invaluable in bringing lectures, speakers, and appearances by liberal Muslims to wide audiences.

Nevertheless, fundamentalism in Islam is fostered as well by division of the world into the haves—the prosperous North—and the have nots—the rest of the world, in which most Muslim nations find themselves. Islamic fundamentalism's influence is also strengthened by reaction to the more blatant expressions of western culture that are perceived as eroding many of society's moral underpinnings. Fundamentalism is also on the rise in countries of the former Soviet Union, primarily in reaction to long-standing Soviet practices: forbidding the construction of mosques, the conducting of Muslim ceremonies, and the observance of Muslim holidays. All faiths suffered from the same policies, but Muslims suffered disproportionately because Islam, more than other religions, governs the daily life of the faithful. During the Soviet period, even some Muslim Soviet Communist Party members who could have managed to bury their deceased in the Muslim tradition (wrapped in a shroud and with their head in the direction of Mecca) were persecuted and harassed. As if the alternative form of burial—in a casket—was a socialist or communist tradition!

The future of Islamic society hinges directly on the interaction of these two currents—fundamentalism and extremism. Islamic fundamentalism can reject the extremist movement once and for all and turn toward a variant of democracy that embraces traditional Islamic values. Naturally, such an Islamic democracy would differ from western democracy, perhaps in the way that democracy in India differs from democracy in the West. But we must understand that for elections, plebiscites, referendums, parliamentary legislation, and something approaching equal rights for men and women to come into being with full constitutional force will take a very long period of peaceful coexistence with religious traditions. Middle East expert Ray Takeyh observes:

> Ultimately, however, the integration of an Islamic democracy into global democratic society would depend on the willingness of the West to accept an Islamic variant on liberal democracy. Islamist moderates, while conceding that there are in fact certain "universal" democratic values, maintain that different civilizations must be able to express these values in a context that is acceptable and appropriate to their particular region. Moderate Islamists, therefore, will continue to struggle against any form of U.S. hegemony, whether in political or cultural terms, and are much more comfortable with a multipolar, multicivilizational international system.[8]

In addition, much will depend on whether fundamentalist movements can resist being hijacked by extremist forces—a possibility that increases dramatically when Muslim populations are seized with the idea of separatism, as happened, for example, in Kosovo or in the Muslim regions of Macedonia, or in solidarity with a Muslim country subjected to outside aggression. Likewise, the equation of Islamic fundamentalism with extremism would be encouraged by the world's division into two civilizations, by the juxtaposition of Islam against the rest of the world community.

While I do believe that there is nothing intrinsic within the Islamic religion or Muslim culture that encourages terrorism, we must recognize that unresolved conflicts, especially the Arab-Israeli dispute, help create a climate in which Islamic radicalism can flourish.

3

Peace in the Middle East: A New Approach Is Needed

The events of September 11 underscored how vitally important it is for the world community to find solutions to regional conflicts. This is especially true for the Middle East conflict, which more than any other has created fertile ground for the rise of international terrorism and its most dangerous forms of expression. In a conversation with Russian president Vladimir Putin, Prime Minister of Italy Silvio Berlusconi correctly asserted, "After September 11, the Arab-Israeli conflict ceased to be a regional problem. Now, the issue strikes at the heart of relations between the West and the Islamic world."

Like many others immediately following September 11, I expected Washington to call loudly and clearly—first and foremost to Russia (as joint sponsor with the United States of the Madrid Peace Conference) and to the European Union and to other members of the world community—for renewed cooperative efforts to end the Middle East stalemate. True, the Middle East is deadlocked in a spiral of violence that neither side can break without substantial and decisive outside assistance. But in this regard, the United States has again demonstrated the unsoundness of its unilateral approach to this kind of foreign assistance. Ever since the Madrid conference, the United States has nearly single-handedly managed the peace process in the Middle East.

Surprisingly, there were no positive signals from the United States with regard to the peace process immediately after September 11. During this time the United States made only weak and unfocused references to the Middle East conflict. One wondered if, regardless of the new situation the world was in, the same U.S. policies would continue, policies characterized by countless missed opportunities to move toward the peaceful settlement of the most dangerous problem, the Arab-Israeli conflict.

In order to gauge the chances of success for the Middle East peace process, we must reflect on lessons that we should have learned from the past.

The peace process in the Middle East began approximately thirty years ago. The Arab-Israeli conflict itself is another quarter century older, if its origin is pegged to the establishment of the state of Israel, and it has roots that go back further still.

The unprecedented duration of the peace process is revealing; even more astounding is the enormous lag between the birth of the conflict and the active political steps taken to deal with it. The world community is not unconcerned; it has been confounded by the consistent refusal of both Israel and the Arab states to comply with many UN Security Council resolutions. The Middle East has been shrouded in an atmosphere of hostility and irrationality. This atmosphere has been supported and strengthened by extremist forces in both Israel and the Arab states. The Arab denial of Israel's right to exist as a nation is mirrored in Israel's refusal to grant the Palestinian people the same right of statehood, although both were established by a UN General Assembly resolution.

The Middle East conflict suffered enormously from being seen during the cold war through the prism of the larger conflict between the two worldviews and two superpowers. The participants themselves sought a way to fit into the cold war standoff. The Arab nations involved in the conflict sought to appear as partners of the Soviet Union, while Israel sided with the United States.

The Israelis and Arabs occasionally trotted out the ideological ties each had with the superpowers. Some Arab nations happily accepted and parroted Moscow's line that they were socialist-oriented nations. There were also plenty of statements made regarding how they were part of the anti-imperialist camp. And Israel proclaimed itself to be an integral part of the free world. All this rhetoric and posturing drew an influx of state-of-the-art conventional weapons into the Middle East.

The situation became more complicated with each new war in the region, as Israel occupied ever more Arab territory. Israel did not initiate all military actions, but it never failed to exploit the Arabs' miscalculations and more serious mistakes—diplomatic, political, and military. Not surprisingly, Israel enjoyed the support of a majority within world public opinion, which sharply criticized the irresponsible calls of many Arab leaders for the destruction of Israel.

These elements not only delayed the start of the peace process for many years, but also made the process disjointed and excessively complex. In addition, because so much blood had been shed, because so many lives had been destroyed, and because so much hate and rage had clouded the eyes of so many, one thing was clear: without active third-party involvement, peace in the Middle East would not be possible.

The cold war did nothing to facilitate a joint effort at positive involvement by the superpowers. The United States and the Soviet Union had conflicting interests in the Middle East—militarily, politically, and economically. Both countries stood squarely behind their Middle East clients. Israel got full support from the West, headed by the United States, while the Arabs received the same from the Soviet Union. In an effort to enhance its positions in the Middle East, the United States succeeded in gaining a foothold in several Arab nations, especially in the Persian Gulf. After the death of Nasser, the new Egyptian president, Anwar Sadat, shifted to a pro-American orientation. This gave the upper hand to the United States as Egypt, the largest and most populous of the Arab nations, left the sphere of Soviet influence; the USSR was unable to build any bridges with Israel. This asymmetry in the cold war also put the United States and the Soviet Union squarely on opposite sides of the Middle East conflict.

Objectively, it was in the best interests of both the United States and the USSR for the Middle East crisis not to reach global proportions. The United States especially feared the direct involvement in the conflict of those Persian Gulf Arab nations that supplied the United States, western

Europe, and Japan with oil. This alone was enough to keep the Middle East peace process afloat through the cold war and gave both the United States and the USSR incentive to involve themselves politically in peace efforts.

Given the realities of the situation, Moscow—and, I think, Washington as well—understood full well that compromise was essential and inevitable. But what kind of a compromise could bring peace to the Middle East? The sides disagreed widely on this, and the key to compromise was found only after the end of the cold war, at the Madrid Peace Conference in 1991: the relinquishment by Israel of the Arab territory it occupied in 1967 in exchange for peace and a guarantee of security. This formula was called land for peace.

The Two-Pronged U.S. Approach

The formula of land for peace is widely recognized as the key to a Middle East settlement, yet it has not succeeded. Partly at fault is the mentality of the parties involved in the bloody struggle over the past century. The path to peace was made longer and its stability jeopardized by two characteristics of the U.S. approach. First, the United States refused to put Arab-Israeli peace efforts above all else. Second, the United States virtually excluded the USSR, and later Russia, from actively participating in the peace process.

The United States monopolized the peace process, but did not devote its full attention to promoting a comprehensive peace solution for the two sides. It must be acknowledged that this approach, which led to repeated lost opportunities, was facilitated not just by Israel, but by the support of many Arab leaders who encouraged it as well through their actions. For example, immediately after the 1973 cease-fire, Sadat described to political analyst and journalist Mohamed Hassanein Heikal his meeting with Secretary of State Henry Kissinger. Sadat said that he told Kissinger he was "finished with the Soviet Union" and now viewed the USSR as "the real enemy. . . . Peace in the Middle East," he said, "should, in future, be organized and supervised by the United States."[1]

When secret Israeli-Palestinian negotiations were being held in Oslo in the mid-1990s, I learned about their contents by virtue of my position as head of the Russian FIS, not from the Palestinians. I was also informed that the Israelis were in consultation with the United States. The first real plan to start a comprehensive peace process appeared right after the Arab-Israeli war of 1973. On October 22, 1973, the UN Security Council adopted Resolution 338 on a cease-fire in the Middle East. This resolution marked the first time a cessation of military action (getting out of crisis mode) was linked directly to the start of peace negotiations. The resolution called for the parties to immediately begin preparing for the Geneva conference, which was to settle the complex of issues involved in finding a fair and lasting peace in the Middle East.

The adoption of this resolution was preceded by talks in Moscow between U.S. secretary of state Henry Kissinger and Soviet leaders. At these meetings, the United States agreed to an approach that departed from its previous position, but that was appropriate given the reality of the situation. For the conference, the Soviet leaders outlined quite a reasonable program aimed at resolving every aspect of the long-standing, bloody conflict.

However, it soon became clear that Kissinger saw the Geneva conference as a way "to get all parties into harness for one symbolic act, thereby to enable each to pursue a separate course, at least for a while. It was as complicated to assemble the great meeting as it was to keep it quiescent afterward while diplomacy returned to bilateral channels."[2]

To justify their course of action, U.S. leaders often said that the conditions necessary to achieve comprehensive peace in the Middle East did not exist now, nor had they at any time in the past. At any particular point, therefore, it was supposedly only possible to make partial decisions, which thus necessarily appeared disjointed. Moreover, those who advocated taking these separate, discrete steps accused the Russians of scorning gradual measures and insisting on an all-or-nothing approach. Rationalizing and accusations like these are completely inappropriate.

In realization of the importance of peace in the Middle East, neither the USSR nor Russia resisted or spoke out against a gradual approach to achieving it. But making decisions in a gradual fashion was conditioned on the fact that they were part of a larger, comprehensive peace program. If a comprehensive plan had been formulated, of course a gradual approach would have been welcome. But any comprehensive measures proposed were countered by partial—not gradual, but partial—measures, isolated and disconnected.

In practice, when Israel faced off against not one, but many Arab nations *and* the Palestine resistance, its separate, uncoordinated actions were arrayed, so to speak, not vertically (which would constitute progress toward a comprehensive solution) but horizontally. This worked to weaken rather than concentrate the overall potential for progress, since each separate act by Israel both weakened its immediate adversary and eroded Israel's motivation to seek a larger, comprehensive peace.

I believe that many in the United States, including high-level officials, understood from the very beginning the ruinous effect that this piecemeal approach would have on Arab-Israeli peace efforts. Indeed, the positions of the USSR and the United States on this issue had moved closer together in 1977. During the summer of 1976, I met with many of those whom President Jimmy Carter had brought with him into the White House. At one of the Dartmouth conferences[3] held in the United States, I discussed the Middle East situation with Zbigniew Brzezinski, later the president's national security advisor. Then two weeks later at a U.S.-Soviet symposium organized by the Russian and American United Nations associations, I discussed the same issues with Cyrus Vance, later President Carter's secretary of state. The two expressed identical sentiments: that the policy of pursuing partial Middle East peace solutions was no longer viable. They both said they thought it was time to work toward a comprehensive peace plan, and they thought that the United States and the USSR should both participate in a coordinated fashion.

In 1975 the Brookings Institution published a groundbreaking report, *Towards Peace in the Middle East*. Among the sixteen authors were Professors Zbigniew Brzezinski and William Quandt, who later joined the National Security Council staff in Carter's administration as office director for Middle Eastern affairs. The main thrust of this report was that a comprehensive peace plan was imperative, but that it was unattainable unless agreement could be reached on the creation of a Palestinian homeland on the West Bank. Two months after taking office, President Carter stated publicly that there must be a homeland provided for the Palestinians. The president also spoke frequently of his desire to resurrect the Geneva conference.

On October 2, 1977, the United States and the USSR issued a historic joint statement on the Middle East. It stressed the need for, among other things, an Israeli troop withdrawal to pre-1967 lines, the granting of basic legal rights to the Palestinians, demilitarization, and the normalization of relations based on mutual acceptance of each side's primary sovereignty, territorial integrity, and political independence. However, the statement drew scathing attacks by Congress and was roundly criticized in the Washington media. Three days later, Carter's negotiations with Israeli foreign minister Moshe Dayan concluded with the signing of a more pro-Israel working document that backed away from the positions outlined in the joint Soviet-American statement. This was the point at which the United States officially turned away (it had effectively done so years earlier) from cooperating with the USSR on Middle East peace and refused to explore ways to achieve comprehensive peace in the region, especially in partnership with the USSR.

Certainly one of the high-water marks in the Middle East peace process was the signing of the 1979 Egyptian-Israeli peace treaty. The breakthrough event could not help but change the essence of Arab-Israeli relations. But change was slow in coming. Even more important, the treaty's separate peace provided a strong alternative to more comprehensive peace efforts. But the treaty itself contained no directives to continue the progress toward peace. Neither did Camp David's parallel document, the Framework for Peace in the Middle East—which Brzezinski appropriately called Sadat's "fig leaf."

The treaty signed at Camp David dragged out the resolution of the Palestinian problem and did nothing to end the fighting and armed conflict. According to former Israeli defense minister Ezer Weizman, Menachem Begin and his supporters saw the Camp David Accord as a "way of perpetuating some form of Israeli rule over Judea and Samaria."[4]

There were no substantial changes in the Middle East peace process for twenty years after the signing of the Egyptian-Israeli peace treaty. Hopes rose somewhat with the end of the cold war, which made the 1991 Madrid Middle East peace conference possible. It seemed under these new circumstances that U.S. diplomacy would back down from trying to monopolize peace efforts in the region and work to broaden the process. The Soviet Union served, along with the United States, as a cosponsor of the Madrid conference (a role subsequently accepted by the Russian Federation as the successor state to the USSR). It was precisely at this moment, when the U.S. monopoly role was eroded, that all the conflict's main figures—Syria, Egypt, Jordan, Israel, and Lebanon—first agreed to participate in the conference. Also, the Central Council of the Palestine Liberation Organization (PLO) approved a roster of Palestinian members for a joint Jordanian-Palestinian delegation.

The United States and the USSR planned the Madrid conference as a series of simultaneous bilateral and multilateral talks between Israel and Arab leaders on general issues. Separate negotiations were conducted between Israel and the Jordanian-Palestinian delegation on the specific issues of the West Bank and the Gaza Strip. The format of this conference demonstrates how the rejection of taking separate steps did not constitute the ignoring of partial steps, but was part of a comprehensive resolution. This was the point of view the Soviet Union and Russia had always expressed.

The Madrid conference jump-started efforts by the conflict's primary participants as well. In Oslo during the mid-1990s, a series of secret meetings between representatives of the PLO and Israel took place. Some agreements were reached regarding negotiations, and progress was made on the issue of Syria, but nothing moved past an exploratory stage. During their contact with the Syrian leaders, U.S. representatives let it be known—apparently with good intentions—that Israel would ultimately withdraw all its forces from the Golan Heights if it could reach agreement with Syria on all other issues. Syria's foreign minister, Farouk al-Sharaa, told me that this possibility encouraged the Syrians. President Assad also affirmed that the United States was, in fact, relaying what the Israelis had said. Soon enough, the situation reversed as the Likud Party came into power and disavowed the Americans' statements. Shimon Peres scrambled to find an explanation, while the United States tried to cover up what had happened and retreated to the sidelines.

Trying to Save the Madrid Formula

At the time Russia held that while progress on the issue of Palestine was important, there could be no peace in the Middle East without addressing the issue of Syria. Moreover, the intractability of the Syrian problem threatened the Palestinian issue. During one of my negotiations with Hafiz al-Assad, I described to him my vision for Syria. He agreed that Syria did not want to be the first to make peace with Israel. On the other hand, neither did it wish to be the last, since that would have left Syria to face Israel alone. Understanding that this dialectic did not leave Syria much room to maneuver, al-Assad said, "We cannot bring peace to the region by ourselves, but we can make sure that Syria is not left to face Israel alone."

In the mid-1990s, especially after the Likud Party came to power in Israel, a swift resolution for peace seemed more and more unlikely. In the situation, the best possible scenario seemed to be not to allow the peace process begun at Madrid to backslide. To ensure this, all sides had to agree on two things. First, to recognize and to abide by agreements that had already been made. In light of the long history of the peace process, this requirement took on strategic importance not only for the Arabs, but also for Israel, which certainly understood the importance of maintaining agreements with an upcoming new generation of Arab leadership. Second, all needed to buy into the need to make progress in many parallel directions at once and to bring all Arab participants in the conflict into the process.

Unfortunately, the Middle East mission I undertook as Russia's foreign minister (to Cairo, Damascus, Tel Aviv, Amman, and Palestinian Gaza) to achieve agreement on these principles was not successful. For the most part, the Egyptian and Palestinian leaders approved of the initiative. The Syrians agreed only partially. And Israel to all intents and purposes simply refused to participate.

My first visit to Israel as foreign minister was in early 1996, while the Labor Party was still in power. Israeli foreign minister Shimon Peres scarcely heard out my arguments before answering, "We only need one mediator, and it is the United States." On my following visit to the country Benjamin Netanyahu was in office, and the situation was slightly improved. At least I did not get any of Peres's stonewalling. But still, there was no progress along the lines proposed by Russia.

In all honesty, I must say that after Ehud Barak came to power in May 1999, the United States made some substantial accomplishments in

Middle East peace. As heavy artillery, President Clinton made special visits to the region and frequently received Israeli and PLO leaders in Washington. The Palestinian parliament removed from the PLO charter a pro-
vision setting the liquidation of Israel as one of its goals. Secretary of
State Albright helped the sides feel out an agreement on the successive
stages in which Israeli troops would withdraw from the West Bank. And
the Palestinian-Israeli negotiations started up again.

Yet all this did not move the peace process further toward any kind of
conclusion. Clinton began to calibrate his Middle East policy to create
conditions in the United States that would help Vice President Al Gore
win the upcoming presidential election. Clearly, another factor was Clinton's desire to go down in history as the man who brought peace to one of
the world's most dangerous and long-standing regional conflicts. For these
reasons his approach to the Arab-Israeli problem was all over the map.

Prime Minister Barak began to take greater notice of Israel's domestic
situation, where elections were also approaching. According to opinion
polls, his chances of winning were not good. For his part, Yasser Arafat
was not prepared to make any kind of radical concessions, figuring that
he still had enough time to maneuver.

In the end, Clinton stubbornly adhered to a line that refused to give
Russia an equal role in the peace process, as envisioned in the Madrid
conference. This decision had an impact on the Middle East summit in
October 2000, at Sharm el-Sheikh. The Russian Foreign Ministry issued
a statement supporting the summit and said Russia was ready to participate at the same level as the other participants. Russia's president was
prepared to fly to Egypt, and he confirmed this with me during a phone
conversation. However, no invitation was forthcoming. Later, the United
States would issue a statement saying that Russia's foreign minister had
been invited to the summit but had decided not to attend. But the issue
had been that while the foreign minister of Russia had been invited, it was
the highest-placed officials who attended from the United States, Egypt,
Jordan, Palestine, Israel, and the United Nations. (The European Union's
high representative for foreign and security policy attended for the EU.)

As the Sharm el-Sheikh summit got under way, the West Bank and
Gaza were locked in bloody conflict. The fighting had begun when General Sharon, head of Israel's Likud Party, had made a show of visiting the

al-Aqsa complex in East Jerusalem. A chorus of supporters claiming Israel's exclusive sovereignty over this holy place accompanied Sharon's appearance there, stressing that a Jewish temple had existed there before the al-Aqsa mosque was built. Sharon's visit triggered a new intifada—an uprising of Palestinians on the West Bank and Gaza. Armed primarily with stones, the Palestinians were met and subdued with gunfire. The number of Palestinian victims was three times that of the Israelis. The negotiation process came to an abrupt halt.

The cease-fire agreements reached at Sharm al-Sheikh failed, and the violence escalated. Clinton continued his solo performance, meeting unsuccessfully with Arafat and Barak November 9–13, 2000. Meanwhile, Russia was following a parallel track—unfortunately not in concert with the United States, as would have befitted cosponsors of the Madrid Conference. Arafat visited Moscow to meet with President Putin on November 24. During talks with Arafat, Putin called Prime Minister Barak and suggested to Arafat that he should talk to the Israeli leader. The two did have a discussion, their first contact since the intifada had begun. Yet the fighting continued, with Palestinian suicide bombers joining the fray. Israel retaliated with rocket strikes, some of which were against civilian targets.

On December 9, Barak announced his resignation. On December 19–24, 2000, Clinton hosted Palestinian-Israeli talks at Bolling Air Force Base, culminating in the announcement of a new American plan. For the first time, it was proposed that Jerusalem be divided: the Arab neighborhoods of East Jerusalem would go to the future Palestinian state and the Jewish neighborhoods to Israel. Haram al-Sharif—the hill where the al-Aqsa mosque complex is located—would pass into restricted Palestinian control, while the Wailing Wall, the Jewish Quarter, and part of the Armenian Quarter would go to Israel. The Palestinians would take control of 95 percent of the West Bank and the entire Gaza Strip. Palestinian refugees would be allowed to return, but only to a Palestinian state.

I believe that the PLO should have conditionally accepted this plan. Clinton's plan was understandably not received well by the Palestinians, but it did meet them halfway. The United States should have stuck with this position and hammered out more detail. Moreover, Palestinian acceptance of the American plan would have made it less difficult for

Sharon to take power in Israel. At the very least, Israeli public opinion would have been affected, and anti-Palestinian sentiment would have lessened. But this was not to be.

Perhaps the Palestinians rejected Clinton's plan because they were influenced by the unfortunate positions expressed by Arab governments at the time. Arab foreign ministers meeting with the Arab League in Cairo on January 4, 2001, and in Tunisia on January 10–11, rejected all perceived concessions to Israel concerning Palestinian refugees or East Jerusalem.

It is also possible that the Palestinians hoped to gain even more than was offered by Clinton's plan in their direct negotiations with Israel in Taba, Egypt. Palestinian contact with Israel continued at a border point in Gaza beginning on January 11 on matters of security. Then, on January 13, Arafat met with Peres in Gaza to discuss Clinton's plan.

It is not out of the question that Arafat's harsh rapprochement approach could have yielded results. Actually, the heads of the Israeli and Palestinian negotiating teams—Yossi Beilin and Mahmoud Abbas (Abu Mazen)—had managed to move their positions closer together during the January 21–27 meeting in Taba than had Barak and Arafat at Camp David in July 2000. In Taba, the sides agreed on establishing borders and made progress on the Palestinian refugee question, successfully separating the right to return from the actual process to be used to put this right into effect. Still, no document was signed. The delegations only scrutinized the notes made by EU observer Miguel Moratinos and agreed to let them stand as an unofficial European Union document.

This was where it ended. Both the Israelis and the Palestinians awaited the outcome of the coming election in Israel, an outcome greatly influenced by the course the peace process had taken.

An Incubator for Terrorism

On February 6, 2001, the Likud Party won general elections, receiving more than 60 percent of the vote.

Ariel Sharon had first ridden into office in Israel on a wave of anti-Palestinian sentiment fueled by terrorist bombers, and he promptly took a hard line against the Palestinians. Sharon said the tank raids and killing of civilians in Palestinian camps and settlements and the destruction of Palestinian homes were simply retaliatory measures. Some people thoughtlessly feel this way today. Others, who may take Israel's side in the conflict, reject such measures as evidence of Israel's hypersensitivity.

Neither opinion is correct. Sharon began to forge his own path, and the acts committed by Palestinian terrorists against Israeli citizens lent direct support to his course of action. As soon as the Likud was first swept into power in the 1977 elections, Prime Minister Menachim Begin named Sharon—a former general who had commanded special forces in the Israeli army and an ambitious hard-liner—to the post of minister of agriculture. This assignment not only gave Sharon the power to establish and oversee Jewish agricultural settlements throughout the West Bank, Gaza, the Golan Heights, and the Sinai; it also made him responsible for virtually all aspects of administering the occupied Arab territories.

Sharon launched an aggressive settlement program on these Arab lands. He was the godfather of the extremist Gush Emunim group, whose stated mission was to spread Jewish settlements throughout Greater Israel, even without any official backing or support from the Israeli government, which was otherwise generally sympathetic to their cause.

In 1982, Begin and Sharon's reliance on physically destroying any Palestinian fighting force made an Israeli intervention in Lebanon the logical next step, since this is where the PLO's main body of troops was located. Speaking before the U.S. Senate Foreign Affairs Committee, former deputy secretary of state and U.S. ambassador to the United Nations George Ball said, "The invasion of Lebanon was not an act of defense. It was an attempt to destroy the sole legal and recognized Palestinian opposition, so that Israel would be able to proceed with the settlement of the occupied territories unopposed. That's the way it is." Ball continued, "In a conversation with General Sharon in Israel, he let it be understood in no uncertain terms that his long-term strategy was to force the Palestinians out of the West Bank and to leave in their place, as Sharon told one of my acquaintances, 'only enough people to work.'"

Sharon's name is closely tied to the murder of thousands of Palestinians—including women and children—in the refugee camps of Sabra and Shatila in Lebanon. The atrocities were committed by the Lebanese Christian Phalangist militia under instructions from the Israeli military.

According to an Israeli investigation conducted under public pressure from Israelis disturbed by the event, Minister of Defense Sharon went to the Phalange headquarters on September 15, 1982, to discuss the cleansing of the Palestinian camps. The following day Sharon watched the bloody cleansing process from the rooftop of a building near the Shatila Palestinian refugee camp.

Armed Palestinian formations left Lebanon, and the PLO headquarters were established in Tunis. Twenty years later, Sharon asserts that it was a mistake not to have finished off Arafat in Beirut. Sharon's unabashed hatred of Arafat stems from Sharon's perception of Arafat as a serious obstacle to his plan of preventing the creation of a Palestinian state. This is why Sharon openly objected both to the Oslo Israeli-Palestinian negotiations and to the success they achieved.

Sharon's actions after becoming head of the Israeli government in 2001 have been utterly predictable and do not warrant particular analysis. During the pre-election period and later as prime minister, he has reiterated his very specific agenda many times. He is nothing if not consistent.

These factual accounts and commentary are not meant in any way, shape, or form as support for terrorist acts committed against Israel. Such acts cannot be justified even as reprisal on the part of the Palestinians, just as there can be no justification for retaliatory terrorist acts committed by Israel. The use of terror against terror has never been and never will be successful. All terrorist acts, whether the work of a single suicide bomber or of regular armed forces, serve to derail Middle East peace and to complicate the position of those devoted to working now and in the future for peace. Each terrorist act increases the overall danger for those living in the region and beyond and sets the sword of Damocles over the moderate Arab regimes who maintain a constructive policy regarding Israel.

Characteristically, both Russia and the Soviet Union have rejected any and all justifications and strongly condemned terrorist actions in the Middle East regardless of who committed them. We always felt that attacks against civilian populations could not be justified by any ideological or political reason. Statements about the price of the struggle for national liberation or the need to guarantee the safety of one's citizens are simply the end justifying the means. Yet this course of action has been chosen by extremists on both sides, Palestinian and Israeli.

I recall in this connection how at the end of 1970 the Central Committee of the CPSU sent Yu. S. Gryadunov (later the ambassador to Jordan) and me to Beirut to persuade the leadership of the Popular Front for the Liberation of Palestine (PFLP) to stop hijacking airplanes. When we asked what the purpose of these hijackings was, the PFLP said they wanted to make "Israeli citizens angry enough to demand that their government enter into negotiations" with the Palestinians. In reality, as we explained to them during this meeting, the hijackings and kidnappings only induced Israeli society to take more and more drastic measures against the Palestinians and turned world opinion against them. Demarches of this nature were not always successful, but this time we were lucky. The PFLP leadership later confirmed that they stopped hijacking aircraft because of pressure brought by the Soviet Union.

Yet Sharon never stopped using terror against the Palestinians, whose territory on the West Bank and in Gaza he intended to annex and whom he wanted to force back across the River Jordan. After the Israeli invasion of Lebanon he said, "Judea and Samaria belong to us. . . . Gaza too, the entire Gaza strip."[5] On a visit to the United States, after meeting with Secretary of State George Shultz on August 27, 1982, Sharon made the following statement: "Israel never has and never will agree to a second Palestinian state. . . . There already is a Palestinian state. Jordan is Palestine."[6]

It could be surmised that Sharon has supported and always will support resolving the question of Palestine with an updated Allon plan (named for Yigal Allon, Israeli foreign affairs minister in 1974–77). The Allon plan proposed that Israeli troops be stationed in a fifteen-kilometer zone along the Jordan River's West Bank (Israel's military border) and in several other locations. Jewish settlements on the West Bank, and access to them, would remain under Israeli control in return for Israel's transferring control of the rest of the West Bank to Jordan. Apparently Sharon modified only this last part—transferring sections of the West Bank to Jordan—to meet his needs today.

After becoming prime minister, Sharon called for the creation of a West Bank buffer zone and agreed to give over nearly half the territory to Palestinian control. Sharon detailed his plan in May 2002 at an economics conference in Jerusalem. He agreed to evacuate a small portion of the Israeli settlements—already widely separated and isolated from the concentrated areas of settlements. Nearly half the West Bank and Gaza would be given over to a temporary Palestinian state, while the remainder would be taken up by Jewish settlements, by strips of territory for access, and by Israeli military units. The portions of the Palestinian state separated from one another by these areas would be connected by tunnels. But even this temporary state, according to Sharon, would be established only after all terrorism had ceased, after substantial democratic reforms had been made in the Palestinian Authority, and after a change in the Palestinian leadership, including the removal of Arafat, had been effected. Sharon foresaw ten to fifteen years of "conditional peace," which could, after the Palestinians had "demonstrated political maturity," grow into permanent peace.

What the present Israeli leadership has done and, by all accounts, what it proposes to do, is alarming. Blowing up the homes of the relatives of suicide-bombers or the homes of members of Palestinian organizations that support them can be interpreted as more than just acts of revenge or attempts to stop the spread of terror. These actions are apparently designed to intimidate a broad section of the Palestinian population into leaving in search of less dangerous places to live outside Palestine. Palestinians are also being barred from the so-called defense zones that separate Israel from Palestine. The process of squeezing inhabitants out of the West Bank and Gaza is also helped by the blockade of these areas, a condition that bars tens of thousands of Palestinians from working in Israel, which for many families provides the primary means of support.

Not the least of Sharon's objectives was urging the United States into war with Iraq. Much points to the fact that the U.S. war with Iraq would allow Sharon to try to take punitive action against the significant number of Palestinians on the other side of the Jordan who support Iraq. I understood the seriousness of this possibility after talking with the prime minister of Jordan at the January 2003 economic forum in Jeddah. He told me that he asked the American leadership about this point-blank, and that they assured him they would never allow it. One must conclude that even the United States does not rule out the possibility that Israel might play this card.

Despite the fact that a U.S. strike against Iraq did put the Israeli population at some risk, motives for supporting the U.S. military action extend beyond just exploiting it in actions against the Palestinians. There is reason to believe that the Israeli political elite, especially the right, advocate and support permanent U.S. military interference in the Middle East to democratize the entire region. When asked his thoughts about what would come after the U.S. campaign against Iraq, former Israeli head of state and foreign minister Shimon Peres, veteran of the leftist Labor Party, said, "The Middle East cannot remain as it is today. There have been—and still are—governments whose time has passed, regimes that have grown rotten. . . . I do not think that the Americans will alter the Islamic worldview, but they may change its habits."[7]

Sharon's solution for the problem of Palestine fully negates the Oslo agreements. It also represents a complete rejection of the peace plan proposed by Crown Prince Abdallah of Saudi Arabia and supported by the Arab League: all Arab governments would offer to recognize Israel, open up normal diplomatic relations, and proffer security guarantees in exchange for a full Israeli withdrawal from Arab lands occupied in 1967. This was an extraordinary offer; previously, the Arabs had demanded that Israel's borders be redrawn as they had been by the UN General Assembly in 1947. This meant without any of the substantial territory annexed in the war with Palestine that followed after the state of Israel was created. Prince Abdullah's plan was completely supported by Washington.

Sharon's plan coincided in time with President Bush's plan for Middle East peace. Although similar in some respects to Sharon's draft, Bush's plan nevertheless did differ from it. Perhaps Sharon had wanted to bring Bush a little closer to his vision for resolving the Palestinian problem?

More about Bush's plan later. Let us first return to the events that resulted from the Likud leader's "innocent" visit to the al-Aqsa complex in East Jerusalem.

Sharon's Dead End

After the outbreak of violence that led to the complete break in Palestinian-Israeli talks, two approaches were proposed to restart them. The United States drafted both approaches, and each complemented the other. The

Mitchell plan was drawn up by an international commission headed by former U.S. Senate majority leader George Mitchell. It proposed measures focusing on renewing trust and confidence. CIA head George Tenet's plan focused on the security measures each side must take to stop the violence. Both plans ran through a familiar list of requirements: a cease-fire, the withdrawal of Israeli tanks to their positions before the intifada, Israel's cessation of settlement activity, the Palestinians' implementing serious antiterrorism measures, and a return to negotiations.

Both the Israelis and the Palestinians expressed agreement with both plans. In reality, however, Israel was unwilling to stop expanding existing settlements and building new ones on the West Bank and in Gaza. Sharon and other Israeli leaders kept silent about this, and settlement activities proceeded apace in the occupied territories. Clearly, Jewish settlement is one of the greatest irritants in this issue. Indeed, by this time violent clashes had begun to break out between Palestinians and Jewish settlers.

Israel did not grasp the Tenet plan's link between cease-fire and the immediate lifting of the blockades imposed against Palestinian towns and villages. Likewise, the Palestinians did not meet the plan's requirement of arresting the leaders of organizations that had claimed responsibility for acts of violence against Israeli civilians.

The renewal of negotiations was obstructed by Israel's insistence on a waiting period to make sure that the cease-fire would stand. Sharon and those close to him surely understood that their demand for prenegotiations could torpedo the peace process. It would simply not have been possible to quickly and effectively contain and block individual terrorist groups from acting. With not only no Palestinian government, but also no negotiations on this point, Arafat was not in a position to stop individual suicide bombers from acting. It would not have been possible to achieve even a minimum level of terrorist containment at the outset without compromise and agreement between Israel and the Palestinians. Such an agreement would have had to first establish a legitimate Palestinian state in the West Bank and Gaza and then to lay out cooperative antiterrorism measures with Israel. This was the only way Israel would have had a chance at achieving security.

In general, the Mitchell and Tenet plans suffered from a lack of coordination, from incompleteness, and, crucially, the absence of any international mechanism for achieving a compromise between the two sides.

As a result, the Mitchell and Tenet plans failed to end the conflict. A kind of internal logic took hold, leading to escalating violence. Bomb attacks were carried out in Israel proper, and Israeli tanks roared into Palestinian towns and cities. At first the Israelis simply carried out raids, then they executed a second occupation of the Palestinian Authority's territory—the same territory from which Israeli troops had been withdrawn after the U.S.-sponsored talks that followed the Oslo agreement. There were civilian casualties. The Palestinian leadership was both incapable of stopping terrorism against Israeli civilians and unable to mount an effective resistance to the Israeli army's bloody acts of revenge.

In late May 2001, as head of the Fatherland–All Russia movement (Otechestvo-VR) in the Duma, I made a trip to several Arab states. I met with Syrian president Bashir al-Assad, with Egyptian president Hosni Mubarak, with the Jordanian leadership, with General Secretary of the Arab League Amre Moussa, and with many other leaders. The high level of tension in the Arab world was palpable but not fully appreciated in the rest of the world. My old acquaintance the Egyptian journalist Mohamed Hassanein Heikal said: "The Palestinians feel doomed, beaten and slaughtered at the hands of those who not long ago were actively engaged in negotiation. This doom permeates the Arab elite. With no hope in sight, emotions in the street run high and spill over to those Arab states [Egypt and Jordan] who still maintain diplomatic relations with Israel. If decisive action is not taken from the outside, the entire region will plunge into chaos." This, I believe, was an accurate assessment.

To this, Egyptian president Hosni Mubarak added: "It is essential that Russia and Europe become actively involved. If not, the Palestinian-Israeli negotiations will not resume. And without negotiations, neither the Mitchell plan nor the Egyptian-Jordanian initiative will come to fruition." As a prerequisite for resuming negotiations, the Egyptian-Jordanian initiative insisted on the withdrawal of Israeli troops to pre-*intifada* lines.

Was there any chance for normalization at that point? I feel confident that the Arab side, including the Palestinians—who were seriously influenced by the Arab world's leaders —was prepared to try.

I flew to London in the fall of 2001 to participate in an economics seminar at the invitation of the European Bank for Reconstruction and Development. While there, I met with two representatives of the Palestinian leadership. My conversation with them left me convinced that the Palestinians continued to see a way out of the conflict in the Mitchell and Tenet plans if only a realistic and manageable timetable for carrying them out could be enforced.

After this meeting, I published an article in the London newspaper *Asharq al-Awsat*, in which I proposed the following. Instead of making yet another round of statements *calling for* a bilateral cease-fire, realistic measures should be taken immediately to start *enforcing* a bilateral cease-fire. Israel should without delay 1) withdraw its troops; 2) publicly renounce any intention of removing the Palestinian movement's leaders and activists; and 3) rescind the order it had given to make preemptive strikes on any armed Palestinians (after all, Palestinians combating terrorists would probably be armed).[8] Finally, the Palestinians must take steps to counteract terrorism and announce what these steps were.

I also proposed that the Israeli government publicly state that it was ceasing its settlement program. With some preliminary agreement, this could have been announced together with a Palestinian statement of agreement to let the Israelis keep several settlements in the West Bank. From a statement made at the Washington Institute for Near East Policy by Dennis Ross, the former head negotiator for the American side, it was clear that the Palestinians had offered significant concessions to the Israelis on this issue at Camp David. Surely the Palestinians would have put this on the table again if Israel agreed to stop the settlement program?

After making statements of this magnitude, both sides would have needed to sit down to negotiations. Clearly, substantial disagreement would have been inevitable at first. But both sides' simply sharing a commitment to the negotiation process could have served as a foundation for stability to emerge.

My article emphasized the need to agree at the outset on two aspects of international involvement in the peace process. First, expanded intermediary roles should be given to the United States, Russia, the EU, the UN, and, perhaps, to Egypt and Jordan, both of which had treaty relations with Israel. The second international aspect of Middle East peace efforts should be the presence of observers on the ground, under the aegis of the UN.

I know for a fact that Russia put enormous effort into breaking the deadlock in the Middle East. This is evident from the numerous telephone conversations President Putin had with Clinton, Barak, Arafat, Asad, Mubarak, Bush, Blair, Chirac, Schroeder, and others. The Middle East issue heavily occupied the Russian Foreign Ministry and entailed many meetings between Foreign Minister Ivan Ivanov and Secretary of State Colin Powell and other foreign ministers. Middle East peace was the purpose of many of Ivanov's trips to the region and of his meetings with the Palestinian leader and with leaders of Israel, Egypt, Jordan, Syria, Lebanon, Saudi Arabia, Kuwait, and Iraq. Yet during this period, the U.S. administration was not inclined to take the active role needed to achieve peace.

Russia did not focus solely on finding a strategic solution for the Arab-Israeli conflict. It also tried to find real-time measures to stave off the escalation of tensions and at the same time to work toward a comprehensive solution. This was evident in May 2001, when, at the height of events, Foreign Minister Shimon Peres visited Moscow. I learned that in their discussions with him, the Russian leaders had stressed the need for Israel to stop its inappropriate pressure on the Palestinians, those acts of revenge that served only to escalate the conflict. President Putin emphasized to Peres that Russia is against terrorism regardless of its source. But when individual suicide bombings are answered with air strikes on residential neighborhoods, destroying purely civilian targets and killing hundreds of civilians, retaliation serves only to inflame emotions and is a road to nowhere. Anyone who thinks Arafat has only to say a word to bring the *intifada* to a halt is deeply mistaken. The Palestinian-Israeli conflict has become so entrenched that mere words and further calls to action are insufficient.

These discussions with Shimon Peres produced two plans for action. The first was to hold one more meeting in Sharm al-Sheikh to establish a new joint model format for the intermediaries' mission. The other was to have UN Secretary General Kofi Annan conduct a mission to the Middle East. Opponents of this plan cited Annan's inaction to pacify Iraq during the time he served in Baghdad. However, in the long history of the Iraqi crisis, military action against Baghdad was avoided through political pressure that forced Iraq to adhere to UN Security Council resolutions. In one case, this was due to a successful mission by Annan. If in the future it had not been possible to avoid the strike on Iraq, it was not Kofi Annan who was to be blamed, but mainly UNMOVIC chairman Richard Butler. His role was explicitly provocative. Unfortunately, proposals advanced by Russia in discussions with Peres, while not refused, nevertheless went unimplemented. The violence continued to escalate. Against worldwide protest, Israel once again occupied Palestinian towns. To mollify western outrage, Israel stated its intent to withdraw its troops in a matter of days. But the troops were withdrawn from one West Bank town and sent into the next. The violence culminated in Israeli attacks on Palestinian camps where hundreds of people were killed.

At the same time, Sharon took action against Arafat personally. Israeli tanks surrounded his bunker in Ramallah, and Arafat was not permitted to leave or to have contact with anyone without the permission of the Israeli military. Sharon announced that he did not recognize Arafat as the Palestinians' leader. In Israel, there were calls to execute Arafat or to forcibly eject him from the Palestinian Authority.

It became clear that Sharon was pulling out all the stops to lay to rest once and for all the notion of an independent Palestinian state. As usual, Sharon urged in statements made during this period that Arafat must leave. But he further asserted that the agreements reached in Oslo and during the subsequent Palestinian-Israeli talks were no longer in force.

Sharon was unsuccessful in his bid to remove Arafat from the picture. He enraged the Arab world, which responded with waves of protests and demonstrations. In Jordan, one protest demonstration was led by Queen Noor. This was significant because Jordan is a prowestern Arab country and maintains diplomatic relations with Israel. The EU took notice and adopted a somewhat harder line against Israel.

On March 12, 2002, the United States and others voted in favor of a UN Security Council resolution supporting the creation of a Palestinian state. On April 14, President Bush announced that he was sending Secretary of State Colin Powell to the Middle East. He also appealed to Israel to stop its armed incursions into Palestinian Authority territory and to withdraw troops from the cities and towns they occupied there. Powell subsequently announced his intention to meet with Arafat in Ramallah. Arafat also received a strongly supportive telephone call from President Putin.

What brought about this shift in U.S. policy? The administration, and Secretary of State Powell in particular, began to consider its need to enlist support from moderate Muslim regimes—the United States considers Pakistan a moderate Muslim state—in the war on international terrorism. After September 11, Bush began to speak out in favor of establishing a Palestinian state and against any actions by Sharon that might draw a harsh reaction not just from the Palestinians, but from the Muslim world as a whole. The motive for this about face is explained by Brent Scowcroft, former national security advisor for President Bush senior, in an *International Herald Tribune* article, where he writes, "[A new coalition can] produce benefits far beyond the principal purpose of running terrorism to ground. It can help erase the reputation that the US has been developing of being unilateral and indifferent, if not arrogant, to others. . . . It can even help unblock issues that have seemed intractable for generations—for example, the Arab-Israeli confrontation."[9]

Although September 11 did result in some shift in focus for U.S. Middle East policy, the changes have been relative and limited. The United States has not reoriented itself, nor has it taken a more measured or impartial position in the Israeli-Palestinian conflict. Any move by the United States in support of the Palestinian position was balanced by pro-Israeli gestures.

Even though Sharon's policies were initially met by an impressive wave of international indignation, he continued to hold onto the idea that he must get rid of Arafat. After vigorous debate during the night of March 3 in the Israeli cabinet, Sharon told his cabinet members he was still hoping to deport the Palestinian leader. He spoke of a mission made up of European representatives that would happen within days to persuade Arafat to accept a one-way plane ticket. I cannot help but recall in this connection a visit I had that same month in Moscow with former Italian foreign minister Gianni de Michelis, now active with the Socialist International. He surprised and amazed me by suggesting that he and I pay a visit to Arafat in the Palestinian Authority. The idea was to capitalize on my relationship with Arafat to try to persuade him to step down as leader of the PLO and leave Palestine. De Michelis felt this would defuse the situation, but of course I flatly refused.

Sharon called Colin Powell's impending meeting with Arafat a "grave mistake." Apparently, he was prepared to express open dissent with the

United States regarding Arafat's future and understood full well that this stance would not cause undue tension between Israel and the United States. Had he done so, Sharon would not have had the backing of many, even a majority, of his supporters.

Without the indulgence of President Bush, Sharon did not try to push for Arafat's removal. Nor did he find support for the idea during his May visit to Washington. On this issue, Bush continued to respect the positions of the leading Arab nations, especially Egypt.

Sharon also could not afford to ignore the situation within Israel. Defense Minister Ben-Eliezer, then leader of the Labor Party, stated that his party would leave Sharon's coalition government if a resolution to deport Arafat were adopted. One way or another, the very real anti-Palestinian sentiment in Israeli society notwithstanding, there was ultimately insufficient support for Sharon's extremist vision at that time.

It also became increasingly clear that continued Palestinian actions against civilians were creating the conditions needed by Israeli politicians and political parties set on derailing any compromise peace process. Arafat understood this. He and those close to him—supported by Egypt and several other Arab nations—made attempts, albeit unsuccessfully, to stop the suicide bombers. At the same time, the Palestinians' actions allowed Sharon to move Israel further and further away from the peace process begun in Oslo. When a group of Israeli settlers were gunned down in Hebron on November 15, 2002, Sharon proclaimed the 1997 Hebron protocol null and void. The protocol had been the transition period's only Israeli-Palestinian agreement and had put a temporary international presence in Hebron for purposes of monitoring and reporting. Immediately, the Israeli government also announced that the plan to restore peace starting in Bethlehem, agreed on earlier that summer, was no longer in effect.

Our Only Chance

In early June 2002, the United States again pushed its own Middle East peace plan, which had become known as the Bush plan. Without a doubt, one positive aspect of this plan was its advocacy of the creation of a Palestinian state as a goal of peace. It referred to Israeli troops in the West

Bank and Gaza strip as occupiers. Both these items represented an offering for the Arabs. The plan called for the permanent establishment of a
Palestinian state within three years, but it also said that its borders would
not be finalized before the end of that three-year period.

This interim state would become a full-fledged Palestinian nation only
if requirements for reform were met and the present government
replaced. From this point of view, the Bush plan looked like U.S. acceptance of Sharon's position, which Washington had earlier rejected.

What possible path could there be to peace in the Middle East given all
these variables? Of course the process should start with a cease-fire. But
definitive success is possible only if an external group takes responsibility
and does more than just organize a new round of Palestinian-Israeli negotiations. This third party needs to work out a compromise plan for peace.

Apparently there is no turning back now from pursuing expanded
intermediary missions to resolve the conflict. In May 2002, the United
States and Russia convened a Quartet of international intermediaries for
the Middle East—representatives of the United States, the Russian Federation, the European Union, and the United Nations. During the Russian-
American summit meeting on May 24, 2002, a joint statement on the
Middle East was adopted. The statement said that Russia and the United
States were committed to using this international meeting to make a
serious contribution to furthering the cause of peace in the region.

In mid-September 2002, the Middle East Quartet proposed a plan for
Palestinian-Israeli peace, the end goal of which was the creation of a
Palestinian state. The plan called for the Israeli troops to withdraw before
the end of the year back to the positions they had occupied before September 28, 2000—that is, before the conflict had taken a dramatic down-
turn. The temporary line to which Israeli troops were to return had been
spelled out during the derailed Palestinian-Israeli talks that were based
on the agreements reached in Oslo. At the same time, the Palestinians
would launch their own war against terrorism.

In this phase, in early 2003, elections were to be held in Palestine. This
was also necessary because Sharon had deliberately worked to destroy—
successfully—the power structure within Palestine. This phase also
included a ministerial-level meeting of the Ad Hoc Liaison Committee
(AHLC) to review prospects for economic development in the West Bank

and Gaza. The importance of this meeting is obvious because Arab nations, particularly the oil-producing nations, could become primary donors of financial assistance for the economic and social development of the future Palestinian state. It is extremely important that Israel be involved in this process in light of the close economic ties it has in the West Bank and Gaza. This is not just a matter of trade, but also of jobs: tens of thousands of Palestinians are employed in Israel. Above all, Israel would be required to stop blockades of Palestinian territory and immediately cease its settlement activities in the occupied Arab lands. A Quartet communiqué emphasized each of these issues.

In the plan's second phase (2003), efforts focus on creating a Palestinian state with provisional borders as a way station to a settlement with permanent status and an end to the Israeli occupation begun in 1967.

This is also seen as a step toward a comprehensive settlement to the conflict "based on UN Security Council resolutions 242, 338, and 1397, the Madrid terms of reference, the principle of land for peace, and implementation of all existing agreements between the parties." The Quartet reaffirmed "the continuing importance of the initiative of Saudi Arabia, endorsed at the Arab League Beirut Summit, which is a vital part of the foundation of international efforts to promote a comprehensive peace on all tracks, including the Syrian-Israeli and Lebanese-Israeli tracks."

In its final phase (2004–05), the plan envisions Israeli-Palestinian negotiations aimed at a permanent-status solution in 2005.

The Quartet announced that it would work continually to monitor the progress made by each side in fulfilling the requirements laid out in this "road map for peace," as the Quartet's proposal was called.

Naturally, the Quartet stressed comprehensive performance by Israel and Palestine on security issues. In this connection, the international representatives called on the Palestinians to reform their security services, to strengthen policing and law and order for the civilian population, and to fight terrorism. In addition, Israelis and Palestinians should reestablish cooperative security efforts. An international conference on Middle East peace would be convened at an appropriate time.

Without a doubt, the new format of this mediation mission gave its initiatives a very positive charge. The Quartet discussed its proposals and recommendations with the foreign ministers of Egypt, Jordan, Lebanon,

Saudi Arabia, and Syria, as representatives of the Arab League Follow-up Committee, and with representatives of Israel and the Palestinian Authority.

This substantial effort was made possible only because the positions of Russia and the United States had moved closer together. Unfortunately, further progress in the Middle East is not a sure thing. Sharon's administration undertook an intensive diplomatic campaign in Washington to get the Bush administration to delay the implementation of the peace plan laid out by the road map. Moreover, the January 2003 elections in the Israeli Knesset (parliament) resulted in Sharon's strengthening his position even further, and possibly encouraging him to hold out against this proposal. Still, if everyone follows the map, a critical intersection will be encountered when the details of Palestine's permanent status are being hammered out: determining Palestine's borders, the status of Jerusalem, the return of Palestinian refugees, and Jewish West Bank settlements. I strongly believe that the international Quartet should not limit itself to laying out the path toward Israeli-Palestinian peace, but that it must also propose to both sides compromise solutions for all these issues in 2004.

Finally, the sole remaining issue will be the enforcement of these compromises on the sides in conflict, by an external third party. It is quite possible that among the Palestinians and Israelis there are many individuals, some in positions of responsibility, who await such imposition of a solution from the outside. This would make a peace plan easier to swallow for extremist forces, which would understand that there was no choice but to accept the imposition of an external plan or risk being left with a bad deal by refusing it.

Opponents of foreign involvement who bring pressure to bear on the Palestinians or the Israelis would do well to remember that the state of Israel came into existence not as a result of negotiations between Arabs and Jews and that it was mandated by the world community. Arabs had to accept the establishment of a Jewish state in Palestine, but the Jews had to accept the creation of an additional Arab state in Palestine. Both groups were forced to accept borders for their respective territories and the status of Jerusalem.

Would it not be possible for the world community to repeat this kind of effort to bring about the creation of a Palestinian state with permanent borders, to determine the future of Jerusalem, and to resolve the Palestinian refugee problem?

The idea of a compromise peace plan brokered by intermediaries and imposed on Israel and Palestine is gaining support. This should not be surprising, since there is no real alternative for bringing the decades-old, bloody conflict to an end. "It should be clear by now that an agreement freely reached between the parties themselves is simply not possible,"[10] wrote former Israeli foreign minister and Labor Party leader Shlomo Ben-Ami. The idea of an international peace plan imposed on the two sides has even been advocated by the Palestinians, for instance, by Sari Nusseibeh, the official Palestinian representative in Jerusalem. Steven Everts, senior research fellow at London's Centre for European Reform, notes, "Maybe the situation requires some shock therapy. Since September 11, Europeans and Americans have an even greater common interest in trying to force a solution, which the parties themselves seem incapable of producing. . . . This document should then be presented to the parties as non-negotiable, and coupled with a binding declaration that both the US and the EU will guarantee the deal."[11] (I will leave the author to examine his own conscience as to why he thinks it possible to exclude Russia as a guarantor in this process.)

When Brent Scowcroft and I discussed the Middle East peace process during his visit to Moscow in the spring of 2001, I felt that our positions largely coincided.

The Middle East peace process has become a training ground of sorts where, in the wake of September 11, the world community—primarily Russia and the United States—can develop heavy-duty means and methods of taking collective political action to resolve regional conflicts fairly and to control crisis situations. Whether this experience will help bring stability to the world in the coming century, only the future can tell.

4

THE U.S. WAR ON TERROR

Resolution of the Middle East conflict would go far toward removing a breeding ground for international terrorism. Despite its magnitude, however, the conflict is somewhat limited in both time and space as a training ground. One aspect of our Middle East peace efforts will stand out as an important measure of our success: whether we can resist moving away from UN mechanisms and toward unilateral or coalition action by the primary players in world politics.

At the end of the twentieth century, this extra-UN tendency led to the use of force outside UN auspices against Yugoslavia, a sovereign nation. On March 20, 2003, the United States and Britain acted without a UN Security Council resolution, essentially ignoring the council's opinion, and undertook an armed attack on Iraq. Is this our first glimpse of a system that will supplant the UN-based world order we know now? Will experience gained from taking individual action to resolve critical international issues be effectively applied in the era after September 11? Or will the principles of so-called humanitarian intervention and an expansive interpretation of the demands of a war on international terrorism win out in the coming century?

The United Nations was a product of World War II. The UN's activities may be criticized, but the organization undeniably played a vital role in tempering international relations and not letting the cold war be translated into World War III. Nevertheless, the past fifty years have witnessed instances of conflict that brought humankind to the brink of disaster.

Without a doubt, nuclear weapons were the main restraining force. Nuclear weapons were possessed by the USSR and the United States, the leaders of two camps locked in bitter confrontation, and by China, which opposed both. Two other powers, France and Britain, had substantially lesser nuclear capabilities and were members of the U.S.-led NATO military alliance, but neither played an initiating role. Thus the nuclear threat deterred these five because a conflict between any of them would escalate into wide-scale war with no winners.

At the same time, the threat of mutual destruction tended to give the nuclear powers a sense of impunity. It was possible to tie their hands, and this did happen, but only in special circumstances. The world did not sink into chaos in the second half of the twentieth century because the leading nations—especially the nuclear powers, who were permanent members of the UN Security Council—took responsibility for adhering to the UN Charter.

Article 2 of the UN Charter expresses a key principle: "All Members shall refrain in their international relations from the threat or use of force against the territorial integrity or political independence of any state, or in any other manner inconsistent with the Purposes of the United Nations."

The right to use force was reserved for a state or states only to counteract an armed attack on another UN member-state. In other words, the UN recognized the right to individual and collective self-defense. In addition, the UN defined itself as an instrument to counteract "threats to the peace and . . . acts of aggression or other breaches of the peace." Chapter VII of the Charter lays out the order of action in such cases. First, the Security Council determines the existence of any threat, then calls on the parties concerned to comply with "such provisional measures as it deems necessary or desirable." If the Security Council feels the parties have failed to comply, it may call on UN members to impose complete or partial interruption of economic relations and all means of communication and to sever diplomatic relations. If the Security Council considers that these measures have proved to be inadequate, it may take "such action by air, sea, or land forces as may be necessary to maintain or restore international peace and security."

At each stage punitive measures against threats to peace are escalated, beginning with the determination that a threat exists and ending with the sanctioned use of force to counter it. At each juncture, the controlling role is played by a collective organization—the UN Security Council. That each of the council's five great powers has the right of veto ensures that one or more of them will not use this function for egocentric interests.

The UN Charter limits the use of force to protect or restore international peace; it does not condone interference in the internal affairs of a state. Article 2(7) demonstrates the incompatibility of these somewhat contradictory principles. The charter states: "Nothing contained in the present Charter shall authorize the United Nations to intervene in matters which are essentially within the domestic jurisdiction of any state . . . but this principle shall not prejudice the application of enforcement measures under Chapter VII."

This mechanism provides the primary world powers with rules of conduct that are largely responsible for international stability. These rules worked during the cold war, but after the breakup of the Soviet Union, the United States was able to occupy alone the position previously occupied by two superpowers. This was made patently obvious by the situation with Iraq during the late 1990s. Supported by Britain, the United States moved outside the auspices of the UN to carry out air strikes against Iraq for its violations of the no-fly zone that the United States had unilaterally imposed. Military strikes against Yugoslavia followed. At a high-level expert group symposium on international law (April 22, 2002, at Harvard University), former Australian prime minister Malcolm Fraser correctly observed, "At that moment, the only resolution to come from the United Nations was one calling for restraint on the part of the United States. However, its goal was not the creation of a better international system, but rather the need for the UN to adopt a policy acceptable to the United States."

That is the way it was. At first, circumventing the UN was accompanied by attempts to extract last-minute tacit UN acknowledgement that the actions were legal. This was especially true with Yugoslavia. In 1999, with NATO support and again unsanctioned by the United Nations, the United States commenced bombing Yugoslavia. The United States accused Belgrade of persecuting Kosovo Albanians and demanded the withdrawal of Yugoslav troops from parts of their own territory, from Kosovo. (NATO recognized and continues to recognize the territorial integrity of Yugoslavia.)

Having not long before branded the so-called Kosovo Liberation Army (KLA) a terrorist organization, the United States and several other NATO members came out in support of the KLA, which publicly declared its intent to break Kosovo away from Yugoslavia and to create a Greater Albania.

Justifying their action as countering massive repression of Albanians in Kosovo, the organizers of the NATO intervention created a situation in which direct pressure from Albanians drove Serbs out of Kosovo in huge numbers. NATO's intervention in Kosovo effectively supported those working to create an extremist Islamic state in the center of Europe. This tumor in Kosovo has already begun to metastasize to other countries, as evidenced by the swift rise of Albanian separatism in Macedonia. Nor did NATO intervention bring stability to Kosovo. Only the illusion of stability is to be seen in Kosovo, not true stability, and it will last only as long as UN troops are present. What happens after they go home?

This entire situation is the result of a subjective interpretation of events in Yugoslavia being given precedence over the UN principle of noninterference in the internal affairs of other states. Measures that served the misguided interests of one nation were given precedence over time-tested collective measures based on the UN Charter.

Apparently understanding the NATO intervention's precariousness vis-à-vis international law, the Clinton administration tried to cast it as not in opposition to the United Nations, but very nearly in synch with the United Nations. Vice President Al Gore assured me—at the time I was prime minister—that the bombing of Yugoslavia did not violate the UN Charter and indeed reflected the general trend of Security Council discussion. How unrealistic this and other explanations were was clear from a statement made by UN secretary general Kofi Annan: "The intervention by a regional organization in Kosovo without UN mandate ended tragically and poses a challenge to the entire post-war system of international security."

Many shared Kofi Annan's assessment. "US domination has led to a true crisis in the United Nations and within the world community. I refer to Kosovo," said Malcolm Fraser. He calls the bombing of Yugoslavia unsanctioned by the UN Security Council "an unambiguous act of military aggression and a violation of international law."

As usual, the UN had to get involved with Yugoslavia. The NATO intervention was not fully effective, and dissent within NATO had grown. The UN Security Council passed a resolution sending an international contingent to Kosovo, and all parties acquiesced. At this stage, a solution was found by forgoing independent action by NATO and returning to UN practice. But does this mean the model for an about-face now exists or that we can be assured it will work this way under any circumstances?

The idea of humanitarian intervention was used to legitimize UN circumvention of the use of force against states later included by the United States in the "axis of evil." Humanitarian intervention allows a state or group of states to use armed force against regimes they feel are leading their countries to conditions of humanitarian disaster. This pertains to wide-scale human rights violations.

The world community is faced with wide-scale ethnic cleansing and mass murder. We face leaders whose policies result in hundreds of thousands, if not millions, of starving, persecuted refugees, in armed clashes with neighboring states, and in attempts to obtain weapons of mass destruction. It is true that in many such cases, human rights and the interests of peace and security cease to be purely a state's internal affairs. Mass violations of human rights and security demand a reaction from the world community, including the possible use of force. But how, and in what form? Based on international law, or despite it?

The main issue here is whether force is used in accordance with the UN Charter, or whether its use circumvents the UN Security Council. A majority of states, including Russia, are in favor of preserving the UN mechanism and have spoken out clearly on this matter in recent years at every session of the UN General Assembly. A minority—primarily the United States and a few NATO members—believes that humanitarian intervention requires a departure from UN procedure. They feel that the

UN process, unwieldy because of the right to veto, only slows down and occasionally blocks the swift action that is sometimes needed.

There might be a real need for certain procedural modifications that would alter that primary international regulatory mechanism, the United Nations. First, however, any such changes should not disempower the UN; it should not be transformed into some kind of consulting bureau. Second, modernization of the UN in line with today's reality should not result from action by a single state or group of states, but through the collective efforts of UN members.

It is easy to see how so-called humanitarian intervention, used in place of the UN process, opens up broad opportunities to justify the use of force based on subjective evaluations and without any of the Security Council's restraint. This could lead to unintended, disastrous results. When President Bush included Tehran in the "axis of evil" and threatened to use force against it, Iran threatened to destroy its oil fields and pipelines in the Persian Gulf. What would be the result for mankind if such an exchange of pleasantries were to be carried out not in words, but in deeds? What if this exchange were the common mode of behavior in international politics?

Many political observers believe that NATO's armed action against Yugoslavia represents a new doctrine allowing the alliance to use force outside its borders even if none of its members has been attacked. This could be extrapolated onto the international situation that has evolved after September 11.

In a conscious attempt to steer humankind away from this possibility, especially in an era demanding united international efforts to neutralize various manifestations of terrorism, Russia has moved toward rapprochement with NATO.

Russia remains staunchly opposed to NATO expansion, since it brings a military alliance right up to our borders for no real purpose. That being said, Moscow has continued the process outlined in the 1997 Founding Act to participate in the creation of the NATO–Russia Council. All twenty council members—Russia being one—focus on projects where NATO and Russia share a common goal, such as new-generation threats like international terrorism. The Founding Act had created a similar council based on a nineteen-plus-one plan.

It could be surmised that one reason the West agreed to this new initiative was the disappointment of many NATO members over the operation against Yugoslavia. One of the more popular west European leaders, former chancellor of the Federal Republic of Germany Helmut Schmidt, expressed the opinion that the handling of the Kosovo-Serbian situation must not be allowed to set a "dangerous precedent."

However, the military attack on Iraq has proved that such widespread European sentiment is sufficient to preclude the possibility of similar operations being carried out in the future. The core issue is that the United States continues to act alone in addressing matters of great international importance.

Even during his election campaign, the younger George Bush declared one of his foreign policy principles to be a U.S. shift toward more unilateral action in areas of security and arms reduction. After becoming president and after the September 11 tragedy, Bush announced that the United States would withdraw from the Anti-Ballistic Missile (ABM) Treaty to develop a national antimissile defense system. The United States also announced that it would address the issue of strategic arms reduction independently, without any obligations, restrictions, or oversight.

This cumulative situation posed several complicated problems for Russia. Despite the breakup of the USSR and periods of serious political and economic crisis in Russia, bilateral (first Soviet-American and then Russian-American) arms control continued through the 1990s. During this period, there developed a considerable asymmetry between the two countries in many areas, including the military. Still, Russia's status as a nuclear power remained comparable to that of the United States, and nuclear parity between the two countries continues to play a pivotal role in Russia's foreign policy. Russia would have suffered a serious political setback had it followed the U.S. lead to similarly reject bilateral arms control and move toward independence in this area. Such a move would have weakened stability on a global level. Joint Russian-American arms control created the very real possibility that China and other nuclear powers would have eventually participated as well.

Even U.S. allies in Europe have reacted extremely negatively to unilateral actions by the United States. I saw more evidence of this in June 2002, in Berlin, at the Twentieth Plenary Session of the InterAction

Council, a gathering of former leaders from all over the world. The majority of presentations, not to mention the conversations we shared between sessions, representing a cross-section of world opinion, were critical of U.S. policy. Significantly, no former U.S. leaders—evidently already aware of what this cross-section would have to say—chose to participate.

The way the United States was conducting its war on terrorism also drew criticism. It was the widespread opinion among the western leaders present—who retain their significance although no longer holding public office—that the United States could test the mechanism of "independent intervention" for *permanent* acts of force against other states. The session's final communiqué states: "The InterAction Council asks citizens and governments of the world to demonstrate understanding towards the United States as it reacts to the attacks. At the same time, the Council underscores the dangers of an exclusively unilateral approach in countering terrorism and emphasizes the importance of the United Nations in preserving the international rule of law."

Truly, not once has so-called humanitarian intervention carried out by a single state or group of states prevailed in the fight against international terrorism. The record shows that neither humanitarian intervention nor even the threat of its use yields positive results in this effort. Indeed, it often serves only to provoke further terrorism.

Neither does humanitarian intervention make any sense as a punitive operation against countries that may harbor terrorist organizations. If such were the case, the world community should give a green light to the bombing of London, where IRA extremists have built their nests, or Spain, from within which Basque separatists operate. It could be argued that strikes should not be carried out against countries that fight terrorist organizations within their own borders, as Britain and Spain obviously do. Yet there are other cases that are somewhat murkier. And who determines the degree to which a particular government is engaged in terrorist support if the UN is shut out of the decisionmaking? These are serious issues.

Putin's Calculated Risk

European reaction to the U.S. withdrawal from collective security measures and strategic arms reduction was reflected at the InterAction

Council's Berlin session in the veiled criticism Russia received for its rap-prochement with the United States. This sentiment belied, perhaps, a hint of envy among the United States' European allies. However, expla-nation of Russia's participation in the U.S.-Russian Strategic Offensive Reductions Treaty, signed in May 2002, was very positively received.

The terms of this treaty were not entirely agreeable to Russia, espe-cially the section allowing the storage of the warheads that would be taken out of service. This would preserve the capability to rapidly reload warheads from storage facilities. Nonetheless, Russia signed the treaty primarily to end the cycle of *unilateral* decisionmaking by the United States in matters of security. It is common knowledge that the United States agreed only at the last minute to give up its position on the issue of arms reduction, which had been to go it alone, without signing any binding agreements and without any verification whatsoever. If the uni-lateral U.S. withdrawal from the ABM Treaty were to be followed by unilateral U.S. actions of this type in the area of offensive weapons, the entire system of international security would feel the effects. Such a sce-nario would seriously affect the actions of Russia and China. It would seriously reduce the possibility of restricting through international obligation today's de facto members of the nuclear club or those who seek to become members, thus damaging global security. This is why Russia decided to sign the Strategic Offensive Reductions Treaty with the United States.

Russia's policy in response to the U.S. retaliatory operation to destroy al Qaeda and overthrow the Taliban regime in Afghanistan was likewise well calculated. The United States chose an unarguably appropriate tar-get for its strike: al Qaeda was based in the south of Afghanistan, and that was also the location of Osama bin Laden. Both he and the Taliban made no secret of their mutual solidarity.

At the time, a few expressed opposition. Some said bin Laden's con-nection to the September 11 terrorist attacks was only hypothetical, a supposition. Others offered that the organizers of the attack could have been Central American drug barons. In parts of the East, some convinced themselves that U.S. intelligence services had been involved in order to create a climate favorable to the administration's aggressive, hegemonic policies. Immediately, Moscow understood this type of conjecture for the fantasy it was.

Soon enough it became undeniably clear that bin Laden had organized the criminal attacks on New York and Washington, and that al Qaeda bore responsibility for committing them. The United States played videotape of bin Laden meeting with his supporters after the September 11 attacks; the tape had been broadcast from Qatar by the al-Jazeera network. The following are excerpts of bin Laden's comments:

> We calculated in advance the number of casualties from the enemy, who would be killed based on the position of the tower. We calculated that the floors that would be hit would be three or four floors. Due to my experience in this field, I was thinking that the fire from the gas in the plane would melt the iron structure of the building and collapse the area where the plane hit and all the floors above it only. This is all that we had hoped for.
>
> We had notification since the previous Thursday that the event would take place that day. We had finished our work that day and had the radio on. It was 5:30 p.m. our time. I was sitting with Dr. Ahmad Abu-al-Khair. Immediately, we heard the news that a plane had hit the World Trade Center. We turned the radio station to the news from Washington. The news continued and no mention of the attack until the end. At the end of the newscast, they reported that a plane just hit the World Trade Center. After a little while, they announced that another plane had hit the World Trade Center. The brothers who heard the news were overjoyed by it.
>
> The brothers, who conducted the operation, all they knew was that they have a martyrdom operation and we asked each of them to go to America but they didn't know anything about the operation, not even one letter. But they were trained and we did not reveal the operation to them until they are there and just before they boarded the planes. Those who were trained to fly didn't know the others. One group of people did not know the other group.

As the magnitude of what had happened became clear, Russia reacted the same way the United States had. President Putin not only expressed Russia's sympathy for the suffering of American citizens but also was first among the world's leaders to pledge to work together with the United States to fight international terrorism. I spoke with President Putin after the September 11 tragedy, and it was clear from our conversation that Putin's telephone call to Bush had been quite unusual. Putin understood the scale of the threat we now faced, and he made a long-term adjustment to Russian foreign policy.

Signs of this were immediate. In Afghanistan, the Northern Alliance—an armed movement made up of the region's Tajik, Uzbek, and Hazara people—received significant Russian military assistance and recommendations to mobilize their entire force and all available resources to resist the Taliban regime. The Northern Alliance had been fighting the Taliban for several years, and their staying power was due for the most part to Russia, which had given them direct support as well as aid channeled through Tajikistan and Uzbekistan.

While helping to jump start the Northern Alliance, Putin also contacted leaders of the Central Asian states that had been former USSR republics. Soon after, the United States signed several agreements for the deployment of air force and ground units in Kyrgyzstan, Uzbekistan, and Tajikistan to "hop" into Afghanistan. Moscow took a very proactive stance supporting U.S. assistance in Central Asia, which was obviously essential for the coming operation in Afghanistan. Had Moscow not taken this position, it would have been much more difficult for those Central Asian states to give Washington the assistance it needed. The fractious internal politics of these Central Asian governments would have been much more troublesome.

President Putin took a calculated, yet nonetheless considerable risk. The presence of U.S. military operational bases so close to Russia's borders and actually within former Soviet republics caused a great deal of concern for much of the Russian public and certainly for nearly all Russian political analysts. Russian aid to the Northern Alliance was not a problem—the Alliance was fighting against followers of bin Laden, who in turn had given aid to Chechen terrorists. But how to make sense of the appearance of U.S. military bases in former Soviet republics? Would they be evacuated after the operation against Afghanistan or not?

And what to make of the U.S. announcement that Georgia was to be a "launching pad" in the war against terrorism and that U.S. military specialists had already been deployed there? If the U.S. assistance was to be used against the Chechen rebels who had lodged themselves on Georgian soil in the Pankisi Gorge, why had assistance not been taken from Russia, which was more interested than any other party in seeing the rebels tossed out of Georgia? These questions concerned many Russians.

We must not extrapolate from a decades-old stereotype that a U.S. military presence near our border must be there for an anti-Soviet or anti-Russian purpose. Yet this persistent misperception of the American military presence was strengthened by the fact that the U.S. operations in these former republics were using military infrastructure that had been put in place by the Soviet Union. In Uzbekistan, for instance, the U.S. Army's 10th Mountain Division was deployed at the former Soviet air base at Khanabad.

There is also a general perception that the deployment of any nation's armed forces, especially within foreign territory, alters the regional military balance and ultimately leads to shifts in geopolitics on a global level.

President Putin decided to help the United States establish a Central Asian military presence for its Afghanistan operation and simply fended off the extreme negative reaction to U.S. military involvement in Georgia. I am certain that this was a conscious, considered decision. Putin took these positions deliberately because of Russia's successful start toward rapprochement with the United States in this difficult fight against pernicious international terrorism.

But how will the United States respond? The U.S. response will determine the direction of Russian popular opinion.

Will Bush's Response Be Adequate?

At the time I wrote these lines, the situation remained uncertain. Few highly placed U.S. representatives were inclined to characterize the U.S. military presence as temporary. On the contrary, on his visit to Kyrgyzstan, where one of the U.S. air bases had been established, U.S. secretary of defense Donald Rumsfeld said that the base would continue to exist "as long as it was needed." This sentiment was echoed repeatedly by others.

As a result of the antiterrorist operation in Afghanistan there has already been a noticeable net geopolitical change to the benefit of the United States vis-à-vis both Iran and China. American bases in Central Asia are now located in close proximity to both the Chinese and Iranian borders. Moreover, easy transfer of American armed forces to any of these bases is guaranteed in any case through Pakistan. During meetings with Jiang Zemin in Beijing early in 2002, I understood that China's leaders were seriously concerned about this development. They feel that the long-term U.S. military presence in Central Asia completes the process of surrounding China with U.S. bases. Iran has expressed similar grave concerns, some of which were raised by President Khatami during his April 2002 visit to Kazakhstan.

It began to look as if the Central Asian governments, too, were not averse to stretching out the presence of the U.S. military in their countries. Some of them sought to use the situation to strengthen their own power and to make their administrations more stable in the face of a sharp increase in criticism from extremist Islamic groups outside their countries and political opposition at home. This works largely because the United States, ever mindful of the value of its military presence in the region, dropped its growing criticism of these governments for their "disregard for human rights" and cut support to their opposition movements.

This may or may not be true, but before Uzbekistan's president, Islam Karimov, visited the United States in March 2002, his deputy prime minister, Rustam Azimov, said in a *Washington Post* interview that the president intended to ask the Bush administration to consider keeping an American military presence in Central Asia permanently. The "Declaration on the Strategic Partnership and Cooperation Framework between the Republic of Uzbekistan and the United States" was signed during the visit. Information indicates that Kyrgyzstan, which at first had sought a fixed time period for the U.S. military presence within its borders, ran up against the hard-line U.S. position and backed down.

It seems that Georgia, likewise displeased with Russia's policies vis-à-vis the former Soviet republics during the 1990s, took note of the pro-American leaning of some Central Asian leaders. This must be acknowledged. Of course there were mitigating factors. For example, Russia was unable to support Georgia's attempts to forcibly return refugees to Abkhazia. The Georgian administration was not pleased with Russia's unwavering adherence to the principle of Georgia's territorial integrity, or with the fact that Russian peacemakers significantly aided in bringing a cease-fire to the Georgia-Abkhazia front.

Central Asian leaders were often displeased with the positions Russia took in some of the disagreements and conflicts that arose between Uzbeks and Tajiks, Kazakhs, or Kyrgyz. Russia was unable to take one side over the other when Tashkent shut off deliveries of natural gas to Kazakhstan, Tajikistan, and Kyrgyzstan, demanding full payment of the debts they had accumulated. Similarly, Russia remained neutral when Tashkent was pressured by Kazakhstan, which unilaterally raised tariffs on Uzbek imports, and by Kyrgyzstan, which demanded hard currency payments for water from the Toktogul Reservoir that it used to irrigate cotton fields in the Fergana Valley. Russia's occasional use of its position above the fray to try to bring the sides together sometimes angered one side or the other in a conflict.

However, Russia's policies not only reflected objective challenges, but sometimes also suffered from a certain lack of refinement or even mistakes. We vacillated too long before adopting and implementing Kazakhstani president Nazarbaev's idea for a Eurasian economic community comprising former Soviet republics. We should have dealt more directly with the fact that the push by some in Russia to accelerate the integration of Slavic republics within the framework of the Commonwealth of Independent States (CIS)—quite separate from the vital issue of creating a Russia-Belarus union—was causing alarm and even protest among some Central Asian leaders.

To varying degrees, Central Asia has been very successful in attracting foreign capital, which now occupies a leading position in some industries, such as natural resource extraction in Kazakhstan. By contrast, the meager progress made toward integration in the commonwealth seems all that much slower.

Collective security for the CIS is likewise an idea that has not been fully developed. Joint border-guard operations at the Tajik-Afghan border and the deployment of the 201st Russian Division in Tajikistan have proved to be fully justified. Yet their success contrasts sharply with the justification for Russian military aid to Uzbekistan to counter the extremist Islamic opposition that gathered in Afghanistan to seize the Fergana Valley. Before and, according to some sources, after the U.S. operation in Afghanistan, approximately three thousand troops of the

Islamic Movement of Uzbekistan (IMU), led by Juma Namangani (Khodjiev), had massed near the Uzbek border.

Tashkent's frequently and loudly distancing itself from Russia or making statements about Russian imperialism did not help the case for Russian military support in Uzbekistan. Tashkent withdrew in 1999 from the Mutual Defense Treaty; it had earlier recalled its units from the joint peacekeeping forces in Tajikistan. But Russia's lackluster military cooperation with Uzbekistan, occasionally affecting agreed-upon deliveries of Russian arms, certainly did hurt Russian-Uzbek relations.

It seemed that any kinks could be overcome by the cordial summit meetings and endless hospitality extended to Russian leaders who visited Central Asia, and by the luxurious receptions put on for Central Asian visitors to the Russian Federation. There was no shortage of warm words, and many important agreements were actually signed. Nonetheless, many Central Asian states turned toward the United States.

This trend could become permanent despite the objective interest both Central Asian states and Georgia have in maintaining and strengthening multilateral ties with Russia. The elite in these former Soviet republics have been educated in the United States or Europe for more than ten years now. Their ranks have already begun to produce a new generation of leaders. Although these young people are not yet in power at the highest levels, their day is coming, and they are oriented not toward Russia but toward other world powers. They espouse a different set of values than those held by many of the current leaders.

This is not to suggest that CIS countries should limit themselves to remaining Russian satellites, especially when Russia itself is strengthening ties with the United States and other foreign nations. We must still maintain a collective approach to resolving the most critical strategic problems, based on coordinated planning and efforts.

The Constant Aroma of Oil

One cannot help but notice that the deployment of American military forces into Central Asia has occurred near the Caspian Sea. Even though the original euphoria over Caspian oil reserves has fallen off somewhat in recent years, the most conservative estimates still compare their size to those of the North Sea. More optimistic estimates liken them to the oil reserves found beneath Saudi Arabia. Putting these enormous oil reserves into production would substantially raise global oil extraction and exports. The United States considers this a priority in order to break the control of the global oil market by the Organization of Petroleum Exporting Countries (OPEC) and to lower prices.

That is not all. Proven oil reserves in the United States are diminishing quickly. The United States is becoming more dependent on foreign oil, which already accounts for 60 percent of what the United States uses. As U.S. oil reserves are used up, this percentage will increase. The least expensive oil presently coming into the United States is from the Persian Gulf. But this region is not felt to be the most reliable.

The presence of U.S. air bases near the Caspian will also be seen by many as an attempt to strengthen the position of the United States in choosing the transportation routes for Caspian Sea oil. In this light, the U.S. military presence in Georgia—for the stated purpose of fighting terrorism—is also quite significant. By all accounts, the Bush administration is trying to dissuade some large American oil companies from building a pipeline across Iran and is lobbying instead for an expensive pipeline (with price tags varying from $2.5 to $4 billion) through Georgia. This option would be more beneficial to the United States and could deliver up to one million barrels a day from Baku to the Mediterranean port of Ceyhan in Turkey.

There is another variation that American oil companies have been counting on for a long time: to have the primary flow of Caspian Sea oil and gas go through Afghanistan to the Arabian Sea coast in Pakistan. According to some news reports, the U.S. company Unocal renewed its activities in Afghanistan after the start of the war. Unocal had been interested in constructing a collocated oil/gas pipeline from Turkmenistan across Afghanistan and Pakistan to the Indian Ocean. After the interim government of Hamid Karzai took office, President Bush appointed a former aide to Unocal, an Afghan-born Pashtun, Zalmay Khalilzad, as special envoy to Afghanistan.

It is hard to resist this colorful characterization from *Business Week*: "American soldiers, oilmen, and diplomats are rapidly getting to know

THE U.S. WAR ON TERROR   75

this remote corner of the world, the old underbelly of the Soviet Union and a region that's been almost untouched by Western armies since the time of Alexander the Great. The game the Americans are playing has some of the highest stakes going. What they are attempting is nothing less than the biggest carve-out of a new U.S. sphere of influence since the U.S. became engaged in the Mideast 50 years ago."[1]

What if the United States were to disconnect its Central Asia military presence from the operation in Afghanistan and to build up its presence in the Caucasus? Even without a public statement of intention, such an action would have a negative effect on the international climate. The very probability that U.S. bases in Central Asia are a long-term proposition causes difficulty for Russia because it interferes with the process of integrating those countries into the CIS. It also seriously damages the CIS Collective Security Treaty.

I feel compelled to point out that Russia has reacted to the changing geopolitical landscape without any of its traditional hard-line eye-for-an-eye response, in either its actions or its official statements. This too is a new trend that demonstrates the desire of Russia's leadership not to harm relations with the United States. But this should not be taken as a sign that Russia will not defend its national interests. Russia will continue to seek new ways to protect and achieve its interests that are more appropriate in today's world. For instance, there is a direct correlation between the establishment of U.S. military bases in Central Asia (a setback to the CIS collective security system) and the measures taken by Russia to strengthen collective security among the Shanghai Six—Russia, China, Kazakhstan, Kyrgyzstan, Tajikistan, and Uzbekistan. (The Shanghai Cooperation Organization (SCO) adopted its charter and set goals in June 2002.) The Russian Federation is also taking an increased interest and role in Caspian Sea issues. For instance, an agreement was reached between two Caspian neighbors, Kazakhstan and Azerbaijan, on territorial border rights to the sea floor. This difficult issue is under further serious negotiation between Turkmenistan and Iran.

The time might also be ripe to pay some attention to the idea of a stabilizing triangle in Asia to provide a framework for greater cooperation between Russia, China, and India. As prime minister, I expressed support for this idea in December 1998. I described not a tripartite alliance—

certainly not a military group—but a way for these three countries to develop and strengthen relations among themselves. At the time I emphasized the urgency of establishing better relations and greater cooperation between China and India, since Russia-China and Russia-India relations did not need stabilization measures.

According to Kanti Bajpai, professor of international relations at the Jawaharlal Nehru University, all three countries fear that the United States could end up dominating outer space with both weapons platforms and reconnaissance capabilities that would give it unprecedented ability to use force offensively. Bajpai adds that the proposed trilateral axis has the potential of building an Asian security system, tackling religious extremism, and using Central Asian energy resources efficiently.

If the U.S. military presence in Central Asia remains and grows, anti-American sentiment will be reflected in the policies of many countries in the region. Undoubtedly, this will have an effect on the energy outlook. Serious damage would be done, as a result, to the stability of the world's energy resources market. Much could certainly be done to counter this eventuality by markedly increasing cooperation between Russia and the United States in this area. Such cooperation would ensure meeting the world's growing demand for oil and gas and could help coordinate and optimize the construction and modernization of oil and gas pipelines. Russia is a geographical bridge between Europe and Asia, and it also possesses great energy resources of its own.

Dealing with Afghanistan Is Not a Walk in the Park

These words belong to former prime minister of Pakistan Benazir Bhutto.[2] Bhutto understands, perhaps better than anyone, the situation in neighboring Afghanistan, long a focus of Pakistani policy.

U.S. leaders increasingly refer to antiterrorist operations as a war, emphasizing the necessarily long-term and multifaceted military action in Afghanistan. Truly, there was no definitive victory in the short term—Osama bin Laden was not found and destroyed, and the possibility of the Taliban's return to power has not yet been removed once and for all.

Before September 11, the United States had no well-thought-out plan to fight terrorism. On September 9, two days before the attack, President Putin told President Bush in a telephone conversation that the leader of the Northern Alliance, Ahmad Shah Massoud, had been murdered. The goal of his assassins was to weaken the Northern Alliance, and further action of this kind could be expected from the Taliban. Although Bush agreed to Putin's proposal for a deputy-level U.S.-Russian foreign affairs meeting on Afghanistan, his overall reaction indicated that he did not fully grasp the seriousness of the issue.

The United States was hindered in developing its antiterrorism policies by its own double standard with respect to terrorism. In any case, the United States has not shown that it understands the scope of the imminent threat posed by terrorist rebels in Chechnya. The fact that the Taliban had direct ties to Chechen rebels and supported them did not receive the attention it deserved.

Before September 11 there was no overt anti-Taliban sentiment in Pakistan, although many there had begun to see that the Taliban was out of control and had begun to act independently of certain forces in Pakistan that had given rise to the group. Ismaili Muslim leader Prince Aga Khan once told me, "I asked Pervez Musharraf directly once, 'What is it you want?' He had no answer to my question." According to the Aga Khan, the Pakistani policy toward the Taliban at that moment was nonexistent, a complete vacuum.

Matters began to change after the U.S. operation in Afghanistan began. The Northern Alliance marched into Kabul fairly quickly. Optimism swelled when reports of victory were relayed back to the United States after successful operations at Tora Bora on the Pakistani border and Taliban positions were bombed with weapons of pinpoint accuracy. But further detail filled in the true picture. Kabul had actually not been captured; it had been deserted by the Taliban, who left their positions without fighting in other locations as well. This was a result of negotiations with the Northern Alliance. The number of Taliban fighters killed could be counted in the tens or hundreds at the most. Others simply scattered and hid. By some estimates, many operations were qualified successes at best: Operation Anaconda, the three operations conducted by the British Marines, and even the widely heralded operation to take the Taliban fortress at Tora Bora.

The Pashtun tribes have not become enthusiastic supporters of Karzai's American-backed interim government (even though Karzai is himself Pashtun). The United States was unable to bring the Pashtun closer to the Northern Alliance—something they had been counting on at the beginning of the operation. Armed forces and special services, which stayed in place after the central government was established, comprised primarily Tajiks and Uzbeks. The Pashtun will not tolerate this situation for long.

President Karzai ordered all political movements in the country to disband their military structure or to give up their weapons, and to send their scattered fighters to serve in the regular army. Apparently this was an attempt to redistribute power, taking it back from the field commanders and local tribes. But the prospects for his success are slim. It is likewise doubtful that the anti-Taliban coalition could use similar methods to easily take leadership control back from Northern Alliance representatives.

Nor has Afghanistan's former king Zahir Shah taken a permanent position in the ruling hierarchy. Brought back to his country after living abroad for thirty years in Rome, he was valued by the United States as a political figure who could help unite the country. Zahir Shah declined to take a leadership position in Afghanistan despite repeated enticements and U.S. requests.

Pashtun who had sided with the anti-Taliban coalition are being systematically killed. Such was the fate of Abdul Haq, who had been an advisor to the former king. Haq had come to Afghanistan to enlist support from the Pashtun warlords but was seized and executed by the Taliban. In June 2002 armed assassins murdered Afghan vice president Haji Abdul Qadir, a Pashtun who had taken a strong public position against the Taliban. How little Karzai's regime had accomplished in its struggle to win local support is illustrated by the fact that his Afghan personal security guards were deemed untrustworthy and replaced by U.S. guards.

Continued bombing and missile strikes at nearly anything that moves led to some regrettable mistakes involving the loss of civilian life. Because the Taliban have largely retreated to the area occupied by Pashtun tribes, many of the civilians killed have been Pashtun. This does very little to engender Pashtun sympathy for the U.S. cause. For this reason, the Taliban find it very useful to locate their centers among the Pashtun. There is reason to believe that the primary Taliban forces are still capable of resistance and are located not only among the Pashtun tribes, but on the other side of the border as well, in Pakistan. German intelligence reports point to this area—between Afghanistan and Pakistan—as the location where Osama bin Laden is in hiding.

There are alarming reports that the production of heroin and opium has increased sharply since the United States began its campaign. Specialists with the UN Drug Control Program estimate that the Afghan opium poppy harvest for 2002 will be ten times larger than in 2001. It is well known that the drug trade constitutes the main source of Taliban funds.

The situation will not change if what the London-based *Asharq al-Awsat* reports is true: that Osama bin Laden's son has been named to lead al Qaeda. The importance of this lies not so much in the fact that bin Laden may be dead or mortally wounded, but that the bin Laden legacy is being preserved in the leadership of a terrorist organization even at the height of the American operation in Afghanistan.

The Pashtun tribal areas in Pakistan have long been a haven for displaced Afghans and refugees. It is not under the control of Islamabad, which fears direct confrontation with those who live in this region. To this day, the border between the two countries is not precisely defined. Since the time of the British Indian Empire the Pashtun area has been divided by the so-called Durand Line, which established a border between Pakistan and Afghanistan. Regardless, neither Pakistan nor Afghanistan sees the demarcation as a working border. The Pakistani position is that this border artificially reduced its territory. And the notion of establishing Greater Pashtunistan, covering some of Afghanistan and a significant portion of the territory of present-day Pakistan, is hardly just a curiosity in the minds of many Afghan Pashtuns. It is difficult to believe that after September 11 the Pakistani government will take decisive action to exert its central power over this area filled with Afghan refugees.

It is symptomatic that during the October 2002 elections, both for the national parliament and regional legislatures for the four Pakistani provinces, the Muttahida Majlis-e-Amal (MMA), a pro-Taliban fundamentalist coalition made up of six Muslim parties, unexpectedly won a majority of the legislature seats in the two Pakistani provinces bordering Afghanistan. Thus the Taliban will remain a viable force for some time in this area, capable of carrying out partisan raids into Afghanistan.

In addition to armed raids of this sort, the Taliban will also be able to infiltrate Karzai's coalition government, which is naturally interested in supporting the Pashtun. Even when the coalition government was being put together, the issue of whether to include repentant Taliban was debated. At the time, the idea was shot down. But what if someone else pushes for it?

It is unlikely that Pakistani president Musharraf—whom President Bush called a "key U.S. partner in the global coalition against terrorism"—could manage to launch an active campaign against the Taliban in his country, even under pressure from the United States. The Taliban in Pakistan enjoy the broad support of many Pakistani citizens, and many officers in the Pakistani Army (especially the special services) are sympathetic to them.

According to a Gallup poll conducted in October 2001, after the United States had begun its operation in Afghanistan, 63 percent of the Pakistani public supported the Taliban and only 7 percent approved of the U.S. action. Right up until September 11, the Pakistani Inter-Services Intelligence Agency (ISI) had advisers among Taliban troops. Surely this should tell us something?

While it is difficult to imagine that the United States would go into Pakistan to pursue the Taliban, the same is not true of al Qaeda. Both the United States and Pakistan are prepared to actively pursue the terrorist group wherever it can be found. Possibly Musharraf sees this stance as an insurance policy against the critics who accuse him of not doing enough to destroy the Taliban. Nevertheless, getting rid of al Qaeda will be much more difficult if the Taliban are still operating.

Based on experience that cost Russia dearly, I would say that the future of Afghanistan depends less on successfully taking over the country than it does on external powers' carrying out multilateral efforts to help the Afghan people establish a federal government. Strong centralized power is not tenable in this country, and the regions must be allowed a certain degree of autonomy, perhaps even to varying degrees. By the same token, the center must be able to maintain the authority needed to hold the nation together.

Naturally, those who understand the importance of the U.S. military action in Afghanistan, which under Taliban rule had become a breeding ground for terrorism, do support the United States. It is revolting to hear those who thoughtlessly malign the United States by suggesting they got what they were asking for. But such comments can be heard from those who have already been through one brutal war in this Asian land and who were deeply offended to hear over and over how unprepared for combat our army was.

It is not important who fights in Afghanistan. What matters is Afghanistan itself, a country that has never been at peace with foreign rule. Yet it is a multicultural nation with a tribal structure, which makes it difficult to foresee any kind of internal unifying force establishing control over the whole. During the Soviet occupation, a unifying force of this kind was sought in Najibullah's nearly all-Pashtun force, wrapped in Communist Party colors. But Northern Afghanistan opposed his regime. In the south, many Pashtun joined forces with the mujahidin, who fought against the Soviets and the Afghan elite who attached themselves to the Soviets. Both sides had wide support from outside the country. In the end, the USSR was forced to withdraw its troops from the country, leaving the lower strata to remain, as before, under the control of the upper strata. It bears mentioning in this regard that even during the reign of Zahir Shah, Afghanistan's territorial integrity was maintained primarily through constant payments from the royal treasury to various warring tribes.

True, the situation in Afghanistan today is different from that which existed during the Soviet occupation. As Benazir Bhutto noted, "There is an enormous difference between the period when Najibullah was in power in Kabul and the present situation. Then, the Afghan mujahidin received monthly payments in the millions of dollars from the US and Saudi Arabia. They had training grounds in Pakistan and received a constant stream of the newest weaponry: mortars, rocket launchers, and Stinger missiles. Who contributes financial support to the Taliban today? No one!"[3]

Bhutto's comments deserve our attention, of course. We should also be cautioned by specific statements made by Taliban representatives and distributed by some of the media that indicated their fighters are regrouping and will be sufficiently equipped to launch a more vigorous counterattack against the United States and its allies. There still is a very real danger that the Taliban's fighting capabilities can be reestablished.

Ultimately, at enormous expense and enormous effort, the United States will succeed in neutralizing Afghanistan as a base for international terrorism. But this would go much more quickly and effectively if all those interested were to join forces cooperatively—the United States, Russia, Pakistan, the European Union, the UN, India, China, and Iran. In particular, it would be useful for the United States to work together with Russia. We have keen insight and influence regarding some of the key control points in Afghanistan. We also have a higher level of relationship than does the United States with both China and India, or Iran, for that matter. The creation of an antiterrorism alliance of this sort is a very real opportunity, since the countries and organizations named above understand how unilateral U.S. action in matters of global importance is counterproductive to and endangers the whole system of international relations, even if such action is directed at antiterrorism.

Who Is Next?

Before the U.S. strike on Iraq, the U.S.-led war on terrorism enjoyed broad international support. Several aspects of this war were alarming enough to give one pause, but they did not predominate and did not cause any major international players to withdraw support from the U.S. effort. This began to change when the United States began to shift its sights away from the Afghanistan issue (itself hardly resolved) to focus instead on carrying out a strike against Iraq for the purpose of overthrowing Saddam Hussein.

On July 22, 2002, London's *Guardian* published an article by Hans von Sponeck, former UN humanitarian aid coordinator for Iraq (1998-2000). Many politicians and political analysts, both European and non-European, agreed with his conclusions. According to Sponeck:

Acts of terrorism against U.S. facilities overseas and the anthrax menace at home could not be linked to Iraq.

Evidence of al Qaeda/Iraq collaboration does not exist, neither in the training of operatives nor in support to Ansar-al-Islam, a small fundamentalist group which allegedly harbors al Qaeda elements and is trying to destabilize Iraqi Kurdistan.

The Beirut summit of the Arab League in March signaled that all twenty-two governments want to see an end to the conflict with Iraq. Saudi Arabia and Iraq have since reopened their border crossing. Syria and Lebanon have normalized their relations with Iraq. Iraq has returned Kuwait's national archives and agreed to discuss the issue of Kuwaitis missing since the Gulf war. Iran and Iraq have accelerated the exchange of refugees. Jordan's national airline flies five times a week between Amman and Baghdad, and hardly a week passes without Turkish and Jordanian officials and business delegations visiting Iraq.

The Pentagon and the CIA know perfectly well that today's Iraq poses no threat to anyone in the region. They know, for example, that al-Dora, formerly a production center for vaccine against foot and mouth disease on the outskirts of Baghdad, and al-Fallujah, a pesticide and herbicide manufacturing unit in the western desert, are today defunct and beyond repair. The former had been suspected of involvement in biological agent research and development and the latter in the production of materials for chemical warfare. UN disarmament personnel permanently disabled al-Dora in 1996. Al-Fallujah was partially destroyed in 1991 during the Gulf war and again in December 1998, during Operation Desert Fox.

"The truly worrying fact is that the US Department of Defense has all of this information," concluded Sponeck.

The United States has not always had such distaste for the Baghdad regime. The Reagan administration, for instance, supported Saddam Hussein's regime, feeling that Iraq served to balance the Islamists who had come to power in Iran. At a U.S. Senate Armed Services Committee hearing in late September 2002, Senator Robert Byrd introduced documents indicating that during 1985 and 1986, the United States delivered to the Iraqi Atomic Energy Commission samples of anthrax, botulinum toxin, and West Nile virus. "I don't think it would be accurate to say the United States government deliberately provided seed stocks to the Iraqis' biological weapons programs," said Jonathan Tucker, a former UN biological weapons inspector. "But they did deliver samples that Iraq said had a legitimate public health purpose, which I think was naive to believe, even at the time." Byrd also described how the United States had supplied the Iraqi army with intelligence on Iranian troops, as well as with tanks and other military equipment.

The stumbling block was Iraq's attitude toward UN weapons inspectors. Baghdad asserted that the UN Special Committee on Iraq (UNSCOM) was acting outside its mandate, and there are many, including some specialists in the field, who agree that Iraq's criticism of UNSCOM was not unfounded. In a July 31, 2002, interview on Radio Sweden, Swedish diplomat and former inspection team head in Iraq (1991–97) Rolf Ekeus said that the United States had tried to influence the UN inspection operations in Iraq and had pursued its own agenda outside that of the UN mission in Iraq. In particular, it sought to collect information about Saddam Hussein and those around him that could have been useful in carrying out a strike against Iraq, Ekeus claimed. He also said that the United States was trying to provoke a crisis in the region to create a pretense for launching a direct military attack.

How often have such scenarios been repeated on our troubled planet, and how little have we learned from them! As Russian foreign minister, I worked directly with the Iraqi leadership in 1997 to get Iraq to agree to let UNSCOM return, including U.S. inspectors, and to comply strictly and completely with the UN resolution calling for the inspection of all items, without exception, deemed suspicious. At that time Saddam Hussein had cut off UNSCOM and sent it packing, accusing the group of overstepping its UN mandate. UNSCOM was led then by Richard Butler, whose antics only strengthened the allegations. Even a former UNSCOM colleague, U.S. disarmament expert Scott Ritter, disclosed Butler's activities on the air with the BBC.

Yet the United States continued to support Butler, a fact they must now deal with. UNSCOM's work was particularly valuable in that the body had been established by the UN to gather convincing proof that Saddam Hussein was not producing weapons of mass destruction. We could not have afforded to risk the established monitoring of many Iraqi objects, monitoring that needed to be kept in place at all costs. In the end, though, the United States had already cocked the gun, and it began preparing for a military strike against Iraq.

Under direct pressure from Russia, Saddam Hussein decided to let UNSCOM back into the country. I will not detail here how this came about; I have already done so in my previous book, *Gody v bolshoi politike* (1999). I will say that during a special meeting of UN Security Council members' foreign ministers (China was represented by its ambassador) on the night of November 20, 1997, in Geneva, Madeleine Albright asked me, "What did you promise to Saddam Hussein?" I told her that we had communicated to him that we would undertake initiatives aimed at changing the makeup of UNSCOM and more clearly defining the scope of its operation in Iraq. Of course, there had been no communication between anyone from the UN Security Council and Saddam Hussein or anyone else in the Iraqi leadership.

That time, President Clinton gave the order to stand down from the attack that had been readied against Iraq, and the international community breathed a sigh of relief.

But Baghdad again confronted UNSCOM in 1998, first temporarily suspending the group's activity and then demanding that it cease all activity within Iraq. This development was used by Butler to withdraw the UN inspection team from Iraq without UN Security Council approval.

Why did Saddam Hussein repeatedly thrust and parry at UNSCOM, advancing and retreating? Butler's actions aggravated the situation, of course, but I do not believe Baghdad was simply reacting to them. Hussein was maneuvering deliberately, delicately balancing his actions to get the inspectors to meet him halfway.

As previously, Hussein's specific goal this time was the lifting of economic sanctions. As outlined by the UN Security Council resolution, the sanctions were to end upon Iraq's compliance with UN demands that it destroy any weapons of mass destruction in its possession and cease their manufacture. Iraq insisted on a detailed schedule for the elimination of sanctions, assuring the UN that it had met all the requirements.

How should we have proceeded then, vis-à-vis Iraq, and how might we have proceeded differently this time, under similar circumstances? Then, we should have made it clear to Iraq in no uncertain terms that the UN inspections team must be allowed to do its job within Iraqi borders and that any action against the inspectors was unacceptable and could not be justified. In conjunction with this hard-line approach to inspections, we should have been more explicit about how or when sanctions could be lifted. We should remember that it is not Saddam's regime, but rather the people of Iraq who bear the brunt of sanctions.

Two approaches were used in dealing with Iraq. One was Russia's unwavering approach: that Iraq comply with all UN Security Council disarmament resolutions and that inspectors move toward closing the four disarmament dossiers one after the other.

The nuclear dossier should be closed when there are no longer any signs that Iraq has nuclear weapons in its possession. I would emphasize that this does not mean the dossier becomes inactive, but that inspection is replaced by monitoring. Naturally, inspection and monitoring are vastly different, since monitoring by the world community could take place with Iraq still having the theoretical ability to produce nuclear weapons.

Next is the missile dossier. I recall a discussion I had with Butler in Moscow when I was still Russia's foreign minister. He was only too willing to answer my question, "Can you say now with certainty that there is no longer a single proscribed [range over 150 kilometers] missile engine or warhead left?" "I can," he answered. I continued, "Then why not close the missile dossier?" And he responded, "You come to an agreement with the United States, and we will close whatever you want."

This cynicism on the part of UNSCOM's chief inspector was fueled by the U.S. approach: that Iraq must provide an accounting of the four dossiers—nuclear, missile, chemical, and biological—all at once, not one at a time. This left Iraq with no light at the end of the tunnel, increased tension, and was not a constructive way to address the issue.

The United States went its own way. In December 1998 it commenced bombing and missile strikes (Operation Desert Fox) on Iraqi territory. The military operation was abetted by a particularly one-sided report Butler had helpfully submitted to the UN Security Council.

As was to be expected, the military strike on Iraq did nothing to move the intractable problem of Iraq closer to a solution. Again, the poverty of the U.S. approach toward Iraq was plain to see: a single-minded military threat—unaccompanied by any political diplomacy—in which the show of U.S. military might steadily grew into the full-scale use of force.

But let us return to the events of 2002. By summer it had become clear that Baghdad could not continue its practice of interfering with the inspectors' work. Undoubtedly, Iraq's fear of becoming the target of another U.S. military attack played a part. On August 2, 2002, after a visit to Iraq by Russia's deputy foreign minister Alexander Saltanov, Baghdad extended an invitation to Dr. Hans Blix, executive chairman of the UN Monitoring, Verification and Inspection Commission (UNMOVIC), to come and discuss the reinstatement of international monitoring of Iraq's disarmament programs. Moscow immediately issued a statement saying that Iraq's offer represented an opportunity for reaching political-diplomatic settlement of the Iraq issue pursuant to the relevant resolutions of the UN Security Council. Similar statements were forthcoming from the UN Secretary General's office, from many other national governments, and from NATO.

Washington, for its part, rejected the offer out of hand and redoubled its efforts to lay the psychological groundwork for a military action against Iraq. This included anti-Iraq statements issued by highly placed U.S. officials and frequent leaks to the press detailing plans for military operations. The goal of this strategy was more than just to put pressure on Iraq's leaders; apparently, it was also aimed at ratcheting up international tension and convincing the rest of the world that the only possible course of action was a unilateral U.S. attack on Iraq.

However, Washington seemed to have bitten off more than it could chew, and, in several instances, the campaign backfired. When the United States publicly focused on its readiness to go it alone with military action against Iraq, in flagrant disregard of the UN, even members of the coalition forces in the 1991 Gulf War refused to go along.

The reaction of Great Britain—the only more or less faithful U.S. ally on Iraq—was indicative of how far the United States had pushed. According to British public opinion polls, 52 percent of Britons were against the participation of their country in any such operation, while only 34 percent approved. One hundred sixty members of parliament— members of the ruling Labour Party—signed a statement expressing their concern over U.S. plans. In a discussion with King Abdallah of Jordan, British prime minister Tony Blair described Britain's priorities: first, to get UN inspectors back in to monitor Iraq's military programs and compliance with UN resolutions, and then, only if this completely failed, to take military action. True, Blair changed his position soon enough, but there is no reason to believe that this significantly altered British public opinion.

The prime minister of Turkey made a televised statement expressing doubt that a U.S. military action against Iraq would yield any positive results. More than anything else, Turkey feared that a U.S. strike on Iraq would lead to the establishment of a Kurdish state in the northern part of the country. In an Associated Press interview, the foreign minister of Saudi Arabia stated that his country "opposed any military action against Iraq." He continued, "We see no need for military action, especially when Iraq is taking steps to comply with the UN resolution."

The Jordanian prime minister strongly refuted a statement indicating that his country could be used by U.S. troops as a staging area for strikes against Iraq. Even Kuwait, a victim of Iraqi aggression in 1990, expressed support for the United States only in the most restrictive and cautious manner. In Moscow for talks with his counterpart, Sergei Ivanov, Kuwaiti defense minister Sheikh Jaber al-Hamad al-Sabah said that his country would not support any unilateral action by the United States against Iraq.

In addition, many U.S. Democrats spoke out strongly against President Bush's blatant disregard for the UN Security Council as the only body empowered to sanction military action against Iraq. Former vice president Al Gore also sharply criticized Bush, saying that independent action by the current U.S. administration could lead to international legal complications. And a U.S. opinion poll showed that 61 percent of Americans believed that the U.S. leadership should consult with its allies before undertaking any military action against Iraq.

The sentiments of many Americans were eloquently expressed by a full-page political ad appearing on October 14, 2002 (following the terrorist bombing in Bali that killed nearly two hundred people), in none other than the *New York Times*. The ad features a portrait of Osama bin Laden dressed as the familiar finger-pointing Uncle Sam and saying:

"I want you to invade Iraq. I am so glad Congress voted to attack Iraq. Go ahead. Your bombs will fuel hatred of America and the desire for revenge. Americans won't be safe anywhere. Please, attack Iraq. Distract yourselves from fighting al Qaeda. Divide the international community. Go ahead. Destabilize the region. Maybe Pakistan will fall—we want its nuclear weapons. Give Saddam a reason to strike first. He might draw Israel into a fight. Perfect! So please, invade Iraq. Make my day."

The ad was placed by one of the private U.S. organization working to stop the slide toward war.

U.S.-European relations were strained. Sensitive Europe was extremely upset by the possibility of a unilateral decision by the United States to attack Iraq. German chancellor Gerhard Schröder categorically opposed the military action against Iraq, and France's president Jacques Chirac called unilateral military action by the United States against Iraq unacceptable.

Under the circumstances, President Bush decided to hold off forging ahead without a UN Security Council resolution—as he had done more than once—on the use of force against Iraq. He spoke before the UN General Assembly on September 12, 2002, using his full collection of stale arguments to support a military strike against the "hated regime of Saddam Hussein." He urged the UN Security Council to reach agreement on the issue, yet he reserved the U.S. right to proceed unilaterally if need be. But this signified a shift in the U.S. position; after Bush's UN speech there were signs that Washington was beginning to emerge from its complete—I emphasize, complete—isolation on the issue of Iraq.

At this point, France, Germany, Russia, and several other countries stepped up their diplomatic pressure on the Iraqi leadership to let UN inspectors back in. On October 16, 2002, Baghdad informed UN secretary general Kofi Annan that it was ready to allow UNMOVIC back into Iraq.

After this, the crisis entered a new phase. Baghdad's unconditional agreement to let UN inspectors return did not satisfy Washington. The United States stated that the issue was not UN inspection, but rather disarmament. This was followed by several efforts by the United States to get the UN Security Council to pass the resolution it needed. After tireless work on a U.S.-British draft resolution, Russia, France, and China succeeded in removing the unacceptable carte blanche it contained for a military strike against Iraq. The final resolution retained the language emphasizing the seriousness of the world community's approach to the critical problem of Iraq and stipulated that, if Iraq violated the resolution, the Security Council would have to consider measures, including the use of force, against Iraq.

Iraq accepted the resolution, and the inspectors returned. According to Blix, Iraq showed the inspectors no hostility and did not interfere with their work. Iraq also agreed to open its skies to UN reconnaissance over-flights, and the Iraqi parliament passed a law required by UNMOVIC making it illegal for Iraq to manufacture or possess weapons of mass destruction. There were no indications that the inspection teams were barred from any of the sites they chose.

Unquestionably, this cooperation was the result of an impressive flexing of U.S. military muscle. Saber rattling by Bush cleared the road for a possible diplomatic solution to the problem, but the United States continued to press, counting down the weeks to the start of its military operation.

Loath to permit a military solution and the serious consequences that would follow, Russia, France, and Germany combined their efforts to produce a joint statement pushing for the disarmament of Iraq through peaceful means. At a Paris press conference, Presidents Putin and Chirac described how the three nations had come up with a way to both increase the number of inspectors and give them more time to do their job.

President Putin emphasized that Russia's participation in this three-way effort was not meant to stir up anti-American sentiment, but rather to help seek a compromise with the United States. This spin was especially significant because at the time three members of NATO—France, Germany, and Belgium—had voted in Brussels against a resolution to provide defensive support to Turkey if a strike were carried out against Iraq. Their reasoning was that such a resolution would only push the United States closer to military action. Even those in Russia (a majority) who agreed with the vote in Brussels understood the risk that this dis-agreement would dilute the unity of purpose the world's powers had summoned to fight terrorism. To be sure, there were some who gleefully anticipated in this a new era of European anti-Americanism, but these individuals were not political rainmakers.

Putin's restraint and Russia's generally reserved policies in this crisis period were guided by the principle that a military solution to the prob-lem of Iraq was unacceptable. Our position was that a war in Iraq would further divide the world along religious lines, destabilize many of the Middle East's more moderate regimes, and weaken the international sup-port enjoyed by the United States after September 11.

Despite all this, Bush forged ahead. Clearly, the circumstances did not warrant such action, carried out in complete disregard of the Security

Council's majority opinion. Bush circumvented the UN process and acted without a resolution authorizing direct military action against Iraq. The U.S. attack was carried out against world opinion—not just the sentiment of Arab nations, but that of nearly all UN member-states—and resulted in an unprecedented level of global protests against the American action. Most significant, the Bush administration, by its actions, had estranged the two countries that set the tone for European politics, France and Germany. For his part, President Putin called the reckless strike on Iraq a grave political misstep.

The Bush administration also seemed to ignore the fact that its most faithful ally, Britain, also received a great deal of severe criticism for its participation, and that Prime Minister Blair may yet pay a grievous political price for his support of President Bush. Robin Cook, Britain's foreign relations minister in 1997–2001, caused a sensation by resigning from Tony Blair's government. Many in the House of Commons stood and applauded Cook's action in a show of solidarity for his refusal to go along with a U.S.-led war lacking international support, a war that most Britons disapproved of, and a war that was opposed by the UN, the EU, and NATO. Cook's statement that Iraq does not possess weapons of mass destruction was particularly noteworthy, made as it was from his long-time position of authority privy to classified British intelligence. A majority of Labour Party deputies—the party making up Blair's own cabinet—spoke out against the participation of Britain's military in the U.S.-led action against Iraq. The resolution finally supporting Britain's participation passed because of votes from Conservatives, the Labour Party's opponents.

Russia did everything in its power to stop the invasion of Iraq. On the night of February 22, when it had become clear that the storm clouds of war had gathered and a countdown to the operation was about to start, President Putin summoned me. He wanted me to go to Baghdad to give Saddam Hussein a personal message from him. I left early the next morning.

Arriving in Baghdad, I requested a personal meeting with Saddam Hussein. At first I was offered a meeting with Tariq Aziz, but I insisted on seeing Hussein, who agreed to receive me at one of his palaces. He and Aziz both appeared, together with the chairman of the Iraqi parliament, Sa'adun Hamadi. I told Hussein I would like to meet with him one on one.

On his orders, we were left alone. I read President Putin's message, which conveyed that if he loved his country and his people, and wanted to spare them from the war and certain casualties that were, unfortunately, about to take place, he should step down from his position and ask parliament to hold democratic elections. As I gave him this message, I emphasized that if he were to announce his resignation, it should appear to be on his own initiative. Russia had no ulterior motive and was simply offering him a way out of this grave situation that was in the best interests of the country and its people.

Saddam Hussein then asked me to repeat President Putin's message with both Aziz and Hamadi present. As I read the message a second time, I was aware that Hussein was taking down my words in a notebook. I admit it occurred to me that he might react positively. I could not have been farther from the truth. Saddam Hussein uttered several phrases that were meaningless to me, clapped me on the shoulders, and left. Tariq Aziz voiced exclamations of loyalty as Hussein exited the room; the parliament chairman was silent.

Leaving the room, I heard the final words from Aziz, "Let us meet ten years from now and then it will be clear who was right—you or our president."

As President Putin had requested, I used foreign ministry channels to inform the general secretary of the Arab League and the leaders of several Arab nations about my visit and its outcome. The foreign ministers of several Arab nations requested meetings in Baghdad to bring their influence to bear with Hussein. Iraq refused to receive any of them.

A few days later the war started, a bloodbath that claimed the lives of thousands of Iraqi civilians. As was to be expected, it was an unequal fight, with the Iraqis pitted against the well-equipped U.S. and British armed forces. Iraqis resisted at first, but after some time their efforts suddenly ceased, and U.S. tanks rolled into Baghdad.

Iraq is not the only country the U.S. administration has in its sights. According to U.S. press reports and judging from the amount of U.S. rhetoric against it, Syria or Iran could also find itself a U.S. target. As with Iraq, many U.S. leaders play to an ultrapatriotic sensibility: they want the public to believe that the younger Bush was able to accomplish what his father could not, that is, to overthrow Saddam Hussein. An attack on Iran would close this chapter, with its unpleasant memories of the failed U.S. military action against the Khomeini regime in April 1980. Their red, white, and blue tone suggests "The United States never forgets!"

A permanent state of war against terrorism is supported by the new U.S. military doctrine, which focuses on preemptive action against enemies the United States freely makes up out of whole cloth. President Bush has expressed this proactive principle in several public statements and makes no secret of the fact that the United States will initiate attacks on countries that it feels pose a threat to U.S. security. This excessively broad understanding of U.S. security jettisons the concepts of both international law and national sovereignty.

President Bush is correct to criticize the idea that the world was more stable during the cold war. Certainly, we cannot use terror and repression as tools to also bring peace, security, and stability to regions that need this help today. But should we accept that the U.S. administration has found a realistic approach to establishing peace and maintaining security in the world? Hardly, if only for the reason that it eschews collective efforts and strengthens the cult of individual, solitary action by the United States.

5

CENTERS OF POWER: ONE OR MANY?

During the cold war, the world was dominated by two opposing ideologies, each led by a superpower—the Soviet Union and the United States. The relationship between the two in large measure determined the international political climate. A third group comprised states that were not part of any military bloc and that formed a fairly amorphous movement of nonaligned states. This status did not stop them from leaning heavily toward one or the other of the superpowers, although contradictory issues frequently forced them to take highly independent positions. This was the case, for instance, with relations between the USSR and China.

The end of the cold war led directly to the destruction of the bipolar world order. The socialist camp, the Warsaw Pact, and even the Soviet Union itself ceased to exist. Many have written that this in effect left the world with a single superpower, the United States, but this does not tell the whole story. Superpower status does not come primarily from quantitative characteristics, although the two leading powers had to be, and were indeed, the most militarily powerful in the world. Size and might alone are insufficient: a superpower had to be able to gather around itself a conglomerate of states it protected and to which it dictated the rules of the game. With the end of the cold war, the label superpower applies to neither the United States nor Russia.

The distinction cannot be overemphasized. True, the United States is presently the world's most powerful and influential nation economically, militarily, and politically. The United States on its own accounts for nearly half the world's military expenditures and approximately three-quarters of the world's military research and development budget. But this does not mean the United States has become the sole nation that determines the course of world events. That this is not the case has been proven by many changes since the end of the cold war:

—The absence of any need for an American nuclear umbrella has made Europe and Japan much less dependent on the United States and significantly more self-reliant.

—Asia has turned from one of the cold war's military and political battlefields into a dynamic focus of international relations. Asia is not a homogeneous system, and it will not become a unified power center. The United States controls neither China (as it has not in the past) nor the new de facto nuclear powers of Pakistan and India. It also has no control over the threshold nations of Iran and North Korea, with their missile technology.

—With its new unified currency, the European Union is comparable in economic clout to the United States.

—China's economic power is growing by leaps and bounds, and its military continues to strengthen. There is little doubt China is becoming one of the poles of power in today's world order.

—Japan has retained its status as an independent economic center and demonstrates a greater interest in participating more fully in world affairs.

—Greater integration within Southeast Asia and Latin America is leading to the establishment of other poles. While not yet very powerful or as clearly defined as Europe, these power centers are making their economic influence increasingly felt.

—Led by those in the Middle East, the primary oil exporting nations (except for Russia, Mexico and Norway) have solidified their position through OPEC as the regulators of world oil prices, upon which depend the world prices of other energy sources. The United States has been eclipsed in this regard.[1]

—The have-not countries of the world, whose economies lag far behind, do not automatically swallow the U.S. line. They are more likely to be influenced by western European nations or by China, India, and others.

—Dissatisfaction with the U.S. tendency toward unilateral decision-making and action is on the rise.

Each of these trends indicates that we are evolving toward a multipolar rather than a unipolar world.

The Effect of Globalization

The mechanism that pushes the world toward this kind of multipolar arrangement is the great inequality in development among nations. Previously, this inequality would lead periodically to the rearrangement of spheres of influence and power in the world through war or other armed clashes between nations. As the world divided itself into two superpower camps and the main players acquired weapons of mass destruction, confrontation between nations continued around the world but did not lead to global cataclysm. Yet developmental inequalities alone were not enough to bring about the fall of the bipolar system.

The end of the cold war unleashed the repercussions of developmental inequality. Freed from the artificial restraints overlaid on them by the two superpowers, developing nations began increasingly to influence the formation of a new world order. This influence is not working toward unipolarity, as might have been expected with the complete fall of socialism, but in the opposite direction, toward multipolarity.

And what of the new process we call globalization? Will increased global interdependence—the greater global interconnectedness in the economy, in politics, and in international relations that is changing our lives—also push us toward greater multipolarity? The process of globalization has been a long one, with specific characteristics at each stage in its development. Today, globalization is fueled by enormous advances in communications that permit the global flow of financial information and make possible agile adjustments to the division of labor on a global scale. Advances in communications and computer technology have greatly accelerated this process.

Today, the United States unquestionably leads in this acceleration process: it is responsible for two-fifths of the global market share of scientific and technical production. This is significant, as the next largest market share in this area belongs to Japan, with 30 percent, and the next to Germany, with 16 percent. The United States is making a serious effort to maintain its scientific and technological lead, which it understands solidifies its dominant role in globalization. But this does not mean a unipolar world order is taking shape.

The world's economy develops through the interplay of three distinct vectors: globalization, international integration, and the transnationalization of global businesses.

Integration is the most regional, localized process and it follows a specific set of rules. Integration does not always coincide with globalization and may, in fact, counteract it. This happened when the EU introduced the euro. But this counteractive effect is limited and cannot be counted on to produce significant change.

Transnationalization is also an independent process, affecting virtually all business and industry today. Although transnationalization would appear to be part and parcel of globalization, the two can also be at odds to each other. The U.S. lead in globalization does not carry over automatically to transnationalization processes. A cookie-cutter approach does not work for transnational development, and the primary capital for the process comes not from one country, but from a wide array of countries. In transnationalization, capital takes on a supernational—definitely not American—character.

True globalization lessens the significance of national governments and can appear to lead to the creation of a single global center in that location where scientific and technological advances are the greatest. Yet national sovereignty is remarkably stubborn, and the world is far from seeing a realization of the predictions of one early philosopher (Immanuel Kant): a global system of governance.

One has to assume that the Bush administration understands these vectors and factors them in to its policies. Yet we cannot assume that the United States is not trying to interrupt the trend toward multipolarity and will not attempt to facilitate evolution toward a unipolar world in order to maintain its dominance.

Unipolar Desires, Multipolar Realities

A tendency toward unipolarity, or at least of ensuring U.S. predominance, is evident in U.S. relations with Europe. For the near future, at least until the end of the decade, NATO will remain the primary western military force in Europe. The United States hopes to take advantage of this to hang on to its political high ground in a Europe without Russia, particularly in light of the waning influence of the Organization for Security and Cooperation in Europe (OSCE). Perhaps this is why the call to sharply decrease the U.S. military presence in Europe—so loudly expressed by Bush in his election campaign as a criticism of the Clinton administration—seems to have fallen off the new administration's radar after it won the election.

The United States is banking on continued NATO expansion in Europe, and, in my opinion, is exploiting the desire of central and east European states to join the North Atlantic Alliance. There are many reasons why these countries want to join NATO and why the United States wants to expand the alliance. Yet Washington's primary concern is not to make former Warsaw Pact states, or former Soviet Baltic republics, happy. By expanding NATO—and this is an aspect of the issue that has understandably been kept quiet—Washington can counteract the European center that gains strength as the EU grows. Although the United States has little power within the EU, the exact opposite is true within NATO. This is why the U.S. push to expand NATO is linked to U.S. policy aimed at preserving the leading position of the United States in Europe, regardless of how strong or how large the EU becomes. Not surprisingly, the U.S. military action against Iraq was supported by the newest members and prospective members of NATO. This tilted the overall balance of NATO in Washington's favor, even as the EU's two powerhouses, Germany and France, remained steadfastly opposed.

Nonetheless, the United States faces a challenge in its bid to maintain dominance in Europe. A *Euronews* broadcast on February 7, 2003, commented that the positions held by NATO's new and candidate-member states regarding Iraq would cause additional difficulties for their entrance into the EU. Over time the lure of Brussels may prove to be stronger than that of Washington for NATO's newest members, so this balancing act may prove to be short-lived. Certainly, there is nothing to suggest any antagonism in EU-U.S. relations in the near future: conflict perhaps, but no animosity. The EU does not want, nor will it want, the United States to leave Europe. This is ultimately not in Russia's best interest either, and we must not base Russian policy on playing the advantages offered by conflict between the centers of power as they take shape. Such policy harks back to Communist Party congresses when international relations were firmly in the grip of ideological combat. Today we seek not to weaken ideological opponents, but to increase international stability. Maintaining transatlantic EU-U.S. ties, however, is not the same as U.S. hegemony in EU politics.

In any case, this seems not to be the present course of European politics either. In its characteristic slow-but-sure way, the EU is becoming a power to be reckoned with not only economically, but militarily and politically as well. This inexorable process is occurring with no formal opposition to NATO. Moreover, it is noted throughout many documents that the European military structure taking shape is not in competition with NATO, but instead complements it. Yet the establishment of a European military is taking place despite—it's difficult not to notice this—the fundamental opposition of the United States. This is further evidence of the trend toward a multipolar world.

It is especially important to see the emerging military and political component of the EU in a dynamic perspective. At the time the EU came into existence, no military role at all was envisioned for it—it was very specifically designed as an economic entity. Then came the development of a common foreign policy and shared ideas about maintaining security without the use of force. This development took place primarily within western Europe—that is, to a great extent within a NATO framework. But this soon grew too limiting. A defining moment was the December 1998 joint British-French declaration adopted in Saint Malo. In part, the declaration stated: the "European Union needs to be in a position to play its full role on the international stage. . . . [The] Union must have the capacity for autonomous action, backed up by credible military forces, the means to decide to use them, and a readiness to do so, in order to respond to international crises." The magnitude of this statement was not diminished by the somewhat obligatory assertion that in problematic circumstances, these forces would be deployed "in conformity with our respective obligations in NATO."[2]

Because of its true implications, the Saint Malo declaration drew sharp reaction from the United States. In a commentary in the *Financial Times*, U.S. secretary of state Madeleine Albright warned against "decoupling NATO, duplicating defense resources, and discrimination against NATO members who are not EU members."[3] However, the EU continues to move toward establishing its own military force. Over the past few years, the EU has developed its own Military Committee (EUMC) and a satellite center to process intelligence data. It has adopted plans to create its own global navigation system, "Helios," and to produce military transport aircraft. The integration of the western European military industrial complex is proceeding quickly. By the end of 2003, the EU should possess rapid deployment and joint military forces numbering 60,000 troops and officers. The EU will have, in the words of Lord Owen, a "separate, adequate defense force."[4]

The U.S. policy on a national missile defense system (NMD) is also motivated by the desire to maintain its dominant position. On this matter, I am in complete agreement with Russian experts A. A. Kokoshin, V. A. Veselov, and A. V. Liss, who write about this in great detail: "The motives for creating a national missile defense system are no longer just military in nature. These systems represent more than just a way out of nuclear stalemate or protection against some hypothetical missile attack by North Korea. What the Americans want more than anything else is something to make them stand out from the crowd in the 21st century's new strategic landscape." The authors see the U.S. push to "maintain its exclusivity" through—among other things—technological breakthroughs in the realm of antimissile defense as a way to avoid dealing with the multipolar world that is taking shape.[5]

Likewise, U.S. efforts to curb the role of the United Nations in the world today and continual assertions of its right to unilateral use of force are obvious and are aimed at interfering with the processes moving us toward a multipolar world order. A more multipolar world is in the best interests of the entire world community—even, perhaps paradoxically, the United States. A multipolar world makes it easier to respond to new security demands, especially international terrorism. The alternative—a unipolar, American-centric world—is already unacceptable to the majority of the world's nations.

It is not unlikely that international confrontation and violence would spread in such a hypothetical, unipolar world. During the cold war, the two superpowers caused no small amount of harm (the question of who was worse is not for this discussion) to other countries. During that time the balance between the United States and USSR limited some of the negative effects their policies might have had. There would be nothing and no one to provide any balance in our hypothetical unipolar world. If this world becomes a reality, the inequality between nation-states will express itself mainly in antagonistic ways. Imagine for a moment, in a world utterly dominated by the United States, the possibility that China might try to wrench free to form yet another pole and center of world power.

This example is instructive in that it shows how there is no interim unipolar step on the path to a multipolar world order. Some international affairs analysts share the opinion that although the current trend may be toward a U.S.-centric world—which is happening regardless of what other countries want—in the future many countries may be vying to claim their own centers on the world stage. This scenario portends a future for our world that is rife with conflict and a return to brutal, global confrontation. As American political analyst Samuel Huntington put it, "a unipolar system would have one superpower, no significant major powers, and many minor powers."[6] According to him, the dominant power in such a system would be in a position to effectively resolve international problems as it wished, and no combination of other powers would be capable of acting against it. The world today has little use for a dominant power of this kind, though no globally dominant powers have ever succeeded in bringing forth a unipolar world order.

6

Lessons for All

September 11, 2001, is often marked as the first day of a new era in international relations, but this is not really accurate. September 11 has not changed the direction of any of the tracks of development of any of the world's leading civilizations. Economically, we are still a postindustrial society enveloped by the processes of globalization and international integration and infused with transnational business structures. Political trends continue unabated: democratic principles are gaining strength within many nations and in the relations nations have with each other, and federalism is gaining hold in multinational states. Culturally and politically, we continue to move closer to a global civilization. And we continue to move from a bipolar toward a multipolar world order. Nevertheless, the events of September 11 were momentous enough to shift these vectors in subtle ways.

This shift cannot be attributed solely to being forced to agree on collective policies to support and direct joint efforts against terrorism. International cooperation to combat terrorism is important, but is not the extent of our international efforts.

I already discussed the need to adopt a charter elucidating the rules of conduct nations should follow when dealing with terrorist organizations and groups. We also need to develop new ways for our various national intelligence forces to work more closely together. This is but a short list of what we need to accomplish. The internal workings of many states must be reconfigured to fight terrorism, and we must become more disciplined as a society. Until now, terrorists have been able to operate much more freely and easily in democratic countries than in their own. This certainly does not mean that increasing security requires decreasing freedom and restricting democratic rights. For any society, including Russia, it is counterproductive to turn the war against terrorism into a threat to democratic ideals.

We cannot repeat this too loudly or too often, for traumatic events always work to the advantage of those inclined to maintain law and order through authoritarian means of governing rather than increased precaution and discipline. We must learn what lessons September 11 can teach us for the long term. First and foremost, we can hope to understand some of the fundamental causes of international terrorism.

International terrorism can grow when regional or intranational conflicts between ethnic or religious groups are allowed to simmer or to escalate unchecked. The vital need to take steps to regulate these conflicts is especially apparent in the Middle East. One of our most pressing short-term goals must be removing the fertile environment for terrorist organizations that exists in this region.

We must also take a fresh look at the North-South relationship. And, despite valid post–cold war assertions that the East-West distinction has disappeared, we must reexamine this relationship too. In fighting against the most highly evolved independent forms of international terrorism—if this descriptive phrase is appropriate—we must root out all its causes and the contributing factors that exist within North-South and East-West dynamics.

An important long-term challenge is to raise the standard of living for the have-nots who compose most of the world's population. This is important. Unlike many political analysts, however, I believe that poverty in the South cannot be counted among the reasons for increased international terrorism. This should in no way be construed as a dismissal of the vital need for global efforts to eliminate poverty in the South. Yet the South is a multifaceted concept. And the roots of terror as a means of waging war can be found in the North just as readily as the South. Moreover, terrorist organizations hardly originate and grow only in the very poorest countries. A more likely cause is the discord sown by the wide disparity between the haves and the have-nots in rights and opportunities. The difference in opportunities afforded these groups often does not come solely from the North's wealth or scientific and technological superiority. Instead it is due to an array of inequalities that discriminate against the South. These inequalities could be ameliorated by across-the-board rejection of the imperialist mindset and double standard that sets different rules of conduct for those in the North and the South.

It is vitally important that the UN draft and enact some kind of international code of conduct for the new world order. This effort could expand in many different directions, beginning with a legal framework to ensure that the South receives the benefits of technological advances and modern education and ending with the elimination of discrimination in all its forms.

Naturally, building an equitable world order requires some effort by the South, too. The South needs to make progress in human rights and democratization. But this does not require blind adherence to a strict Northern model, in disregard for local history and tradition.

Now is the time to reevaluate and re-think the East-West relationship. Membership in one or the other of these two groups has always been determined by politics rather than geography. By the end of the twentieth century the distinction between East and West had largely disappeared. Even after the cold war, we might need to consider keeping this useful distinction somewhat intact with respect to the bicentricism that still exists in the area of strategic nuclear weapons.

Under the circumstances, what can we do to provide a united, cohesive counterforce against terrorism?

First, a few hard and fast truths:

—Infusing international relations with a new spirit will not be helped by unilateral independent action—even by the world's strongest power—but by global unity and cooperation.

—Healthy powers must not base their interactions on religious or cultural principles. Neither must they swallow all the values—or share all the views—of others who lead antiterrorist efforts. In other words, they must not unquestioningly follow a leader regardless of the direction.

—Consensus and cooperation are requisites for a strong antiterrorist front. Nations, especially if they are major world powers, must use methods that do not run counter to the interests of others when they work to ensure their own security and the security of others. The world should guard against any power's returning to the practice of a zero-sum game. In the past, both Russia and the United States often acted in this way, in which a win or a loss for one side resulted in the opposite for the other. Today, under drastically different circumstances, we have a wide array of shared interests, one of which is to protect ourselves against terrorism. This leads to a broad platform on which we can work to resolve the problems the world faces. Yet we must be able to constantly adjust our approach to these problems, particularly in such sensitive and critical areas as security.

The Thorny Issue of Security

In matters of security, I see a crucial need to reach agreement on three interrelated issues: the militarization of space, antimissile systems, and nuclear nonproliferation. The new world we live in should influence our vision for these challenges and their solutions. It should tell us something that after the September 11 attacks on New York and Washington, the number of Americans favoring military spending on antimissile defense over other kinds of weapons spending decreased sharply. Participants in a *Newsweek* poll conducted right after September 11 were in favor of new approaches in U.S. military policy and practice by a margin of 71 percent to 18 percent.[1]

Militarization of space is not a new issue. But the need for us to reject development in this area is now more acute than ever. If we let the opportunity to bring this about slip through our grasp, humankind will face a long-term, intractable strategic problem. Time is also of the essence because the United States has announced its intention to develop a space-based antimissile defense system. Not only does this have nothing to do with efforts against terrorism, but it exacerbates these efforts by dividing nations and setting their interests at odds. There are two variations for which this conclusion is equally valid. If the United States were to use its enormous economic and technological resources to establish superiority in the militarization of space, other states would be powerless to present any competition. Then the United States would have a monopoly not only in missile defense, but also in a new strategic offensive space-to-earth weapons system and a space-based anti-satellite system. This would fundamentally change the world's present military and political balance. With no real opponents to the United States in the world today, such a situation would only encourage those in the United States who advocate more unilateral U.S. action and perhaps the use of force not only against rogue states.

A second variation would be that other industrially and technologically advanced states would seek to block the U.S. monopoly in space by developing and deploying their own space-based weapons, thereby causing the arms race to soar into space with unforeseeable consequences. How could this possibly help strengthen international security in the twenty-first century, or even ensure the security of just the United States?

History has already tried to teach us this lesson. There was a time when the USSR and the United States had enough sense and enough will to keep the arms race out of space. The United States conducted nine nuclear tests in space from August 1958 to November 1962. The Soviet Union, too, conducted four nuclear tests in space in 1961–62. The goal of this and other testing was to perfect the use of nuclear explosions in space to neutralize the ballistic missiles of a supposed opponent. These and other experiments significantly disturbed the Earth's magnetic field and littered the space around our planet with junk. Both the United States and the USSR realized that continued testing could interfere with the normal operation of near-Earth satellites and seriously damage the civil and military communications systems that used them. Worse, it could distort electronic transmissions and knock out nuclear early-warning systems. During the cold war this posed a dire threat. Nuclear explosions in space would have closed off huge zones to manned space flight.

At that time, the United States and the USSR agreed to a mutual moratorium on nuclear testing in space, opening it up instead to scientific and commercial use. The passive military use of space was not excluded: for example, putting into orbit intelligence-gathering satellites and tracking and monitoring equipment. In 1963 the United States and the USSR signed the Treaty Banning Nuclear Weapon Tests in the Atmosphere, in Outer Space and Under Water. In 1967, the Soviet Union and the United States concluded the Outer Space Treaty, which banned the placement of weapons of mass destruction in space and was open to signing by any other states as well. The Strategic Arms Limitation Talks (SALT I) and Anti-Ballistic Missile (ABM) treaties broadened these restrictions: we agreed not to interfere with each other's space-based monitoring systems and not to place into space or to test in space national missile defense systems. As a result, our two states continued to put satellites—including military satellites—into orbit. But to this day weapons have not been deployed in space, which has remained, like Antarctica, a demilitarized zone.

However, attempts to turn space into an active military environment did continue, even progressing beyond the planning stage for partially space-based NMD. In January 2001, the second Rumsfeld commission (the so-called Space Commission)—headed by Donald Rumsfeld, now U.S. secretary of defense—published a report for the U.S. Congress urging a reevaluation of space-based deployment of U.S. weapons "for the defense of our satellites and space assets."[2] The commission's recommendations opened the doors for an arms race in space and could constitute serious obstacles to national and international scientific and commercial space programs.

The Rumsfeld commission's recommendations drew wide criticism even from within the United States, with some Democratic senators speaking out sharply against its findings. American plans to militarize space slowed, ostensibly for technical and financial reasons. But this does not mean the issue is no longer an urgent one; the time is now to reach agreement on keeping space free of weapons.

The answer lies not, it seems, in simply banning NMD outright. Clearly, we must undertake consultations on NMD research and development that would allow us to restrict the active use of space for military purposes. We have already had some success in this direction. In the 1990s, Russian and U.S. specialists meeting in Geneva were able to agree on a demarcation line for low-speed strategic and tactical NMD. In 1997 in Helsinki, I participated in an effort to identify criteria to be used for establishing barriers to the development of strategic NMD. Among them was a ban on space-based interceptors. The United States and Russia adopted in Helsinki a methodology for dealing with the inevitable scientific and technological advances that await us. This important agreement stipulated that as each side made certain technological breakthroughs, it would consult with the other to reach agreements appropriate for the new conditions.

Madeleine Albright and I signed the agreement containing these vital conditions in New York in September that same year. I will not pretend that the Helsinki negotiations went smoothly. But with the participation of military specialists from both sides, we were able to reach an agreement acceptable to both the United States and Russia. Surely this positive experience—which ultimately tipped the scales in favor of SALT II's ratification by the Duma—demonstrates how much can be accomplished through a bilateral approach.

Apparently, the solution also does not lie in banning the passive military use of space. The train, as they say, has left the station on this one. Anyway, banning the deployment of military monitoring systems would undermine the system of restraint. We must come up with ways not to destroy, but to adapt this system to reflect both the familiar threats *and* the new threats we so clearly face after the cold war. Among the means of accomplishing this that Russia has proposed is the collective development of antimissile systems to protect not just the United States but also other parts of the world—Europe and Asia—from possible nuclear attack. Developing these systems collectively would take advantage of the intellectual resources and technology possessed by countries other than the United States and, extremely important, it would eliminate the suspicion that NMD would be used in the interests of only one country.

At the same time, it would be worthwhile to concentrate on developing nonnuclear, non-space-based measures to protect military space assets used for tracking and monitoring from attacks aimed at destroying them or at interfering with their operation. Such measures could include a ban on antisatellite systems based not only in space, but on land, at sea, and in the air as well.

To bring antiterrorism efforts closer together, it is important that one power alone not build up new kinds of weaponry or monopolize the move into space while challenging others to compete with it in this as yet nonmilitarized sphere. What we need is the kind of well-thought-out and organic agreement embodied by the 1967 Outer Space Treaty. An agreement of this type could be joined by all countries with an interest in preserving scientific and commercial access to space. The number of countries directly or indirectly interested in this would grow, thus creating yet another basis on which the world community would come closer together.

This is the approach we must use to address the ABM treaty. Much has been written and said about the need to preserve this treaty and to honor it. Apparently, a majority of countries, many of whom are NATO members, are prepared to do so. They share an understanding of how important this keystone treaty is for strategic stability today and how it could serve as the primary deterrent to a renewed arms race.

I will not belabor the point here; it has already been widely addressed. Still, the events of September 11 are relevant to one of the ABM treaty's primary selling points: its positive influence on the nonproliferation of nuclear weapons. Non-proliferation has always been closely tied to the disarmament process. One of the prime arguments in favor of new countries' acquiring nuclear weapons is the oft-repeated assertion that they need nuclear weapons because there has not yet been full nuclear disarmament. Although getting up to speed on full disarmament is not an easy goal, the first steps toward it were laid out in the ABM treaty. The preamble of the treaty simply and directly underscores the following goal: "to achieve at the earliest possible date the cessation of the nuclear arms race and to take effective measures toward reductions in strategic arms, nuclear disarmament, and general and complete disarmament."

We have not gone far enough in this direction. But the ABM treaty constituted a necessary prerequisite for the signing of SALT I, SALT II, and the Intermediate Range Nuclear Forces (INF) Treaty—for taking nuclear disarmament from theory to reality. This alone gives all countries, without exception, an interest in the fate of the ABM treaty.

This issue has one other important aspect. The United States announced its abrogation of the ABM treaty in blatant disregard of the overwhelming majority of world opinion. And it did so just at the moment Russia had retreated from its previous position that the treaty was inviolate. Russia was prepared to work toward a compromise with the United States and had agreed to discussions aimed at preserving the treaty with mutually acceptable changes. I think the motive for this shift in Russia's position was not simply to try and stop the United States from making such a rash decision, or to save this important international agreement and preserve the stabilizing effect it has on the world. I think Russia feared that destroying the ABM treaty would engender a mutinous attitude toward other international obligations. Such an attitude is exactly the opposite of what we need now, as we try to support antiterrorist efforts with new national obligations and responsibilities that might, as we have mentioned, be best fixed in a charter of some kind.

Let us return to nonproliferation of WMD, a topic that ranges far wider than the ABM treaty, no matter how important that document is.

The nuclear club's expansion at the end of the twentieth century did not happen out of a clear blue sky. Threshold and pre-threshold nations were discussed in detail in two unclassified reports prepared by the Russian Foreign Intelligence Service (FIS) in 1992 and 1995. The reports outlined criteria that could be used to determine how close a threshold or pre-threshold state was to having nuclear weapons capability. The reports attracted some international attention and formed the basis for useful discussions and analysis between the FIS, the Central Intelligence Agency (CIA), and several other intelligence services. But we did not manage to stop nuclear weapons from proliferating.

Do we even possess the means to stop the process of proliferation? This is not an idle question. Whether we find the means to stop nuclear weapons proliferation will determine in large part how successful we are in maintaining international stability.

The Comprehensive Test Ban treaty was signed in 1963 and the Nuclear Non-Proliferation Treaty was signed in 1968. Although these significant treaties had a positive effect, we must acknowledge that they did not stop the number of nuclear powers from increasing. When some states simply did not join the treaties, the world did not react nearly as strongly as it should have.

So what now, as we go forward? To return India, Pakistan, and Israel to their prenuclear status in today's world is not possible. Barring that, eliminating the regional conflicts these countries are involved in would represent an enormously significant step. One thing we can try to do immediately is develop measures that would sharply increase the consequences for using nuclear weapons or for selling them to others. Likewise, there must be penalties for violating the ban on distributing documentation and technology to countries trying to acquire nuclear weapons.

Measures must also be developed for the threshold and pre-threshold nations. The time has come—September 11 was our wake-up call—to mobilize every intellectual resource and involve the major world powers to do everything in our power to stop nuclear proliferation. It is not likely that we will be able to completely stop the spread of nuclear weapons. But we can try to make obtaining nuclear weapons more difficult; we can slow the process. This will help until a time when, perhaps, the world is less volatile. Today, it should be clear to all that "everything in our power" cannot include the use of military force against those who seek entrance into the nuclear club. Quite simply, the consequences could be catastrophic.

Undoubtedly, the threat of nuclear proliferation would be easier to deal with if we could eliminate the international conflicts that grip the countries seeking to acquire nuclear weapons or other kinds of WMD. By the same token, it complicates the resolution of these issues to pin labels on such countries and assign them to some arbitrary axis of evil.

Nonproliferation efforts would be helped by assisting the have-not nations of the world with financing and technology to use atomic energy for peaceful purposes. Aid of this kind would induce these countries to sign on to the established international legal framework forbidding the military spin-off that often results from nuclear power programs. And the opposite—discriminatory measures or sanctions as a reaction to nuclear power plant construction condoned under international (IAEA) oversight or disincentives for nuclear research and development—will induce these countries to seek their own back-door routes to full nuclear status outside of any control.

One of the ways we can stave off the rush of new countries to acquire nuclear weapons is to change the fact that the five declared nuclear powers serve as the permanent members of the UN Security Council, the acme of global policymaking. It is high time to reform the UN structure, but the task must be done with the utmost caution so as not to undermine the body's peacemaking functions. I feel that UN Security Council reform can and should be accomplished without changing the UN Charter. Only this will ensure that the UN does not become an ineffectual organization unable to hold back the destructive forces at work in today's world.

7

Russia's Role in the Contemporary World

The place a country holds in the world is determined by many factors. In Russia's case, the difficulty of predicting the course of our economic development has become the key factor in uncertainty over what role Russia will play in the world. Generally, we feel we can rely on our unique combination of riches: mineral wealth, the intellectual potential of our population, and our immense land mass. But how are these undisputed assets best engaged to benefit our economy?

It is clear that the policies adopted during the 1990s are not the way to proceed. During this period our resources were not used very effectively at all, in fact. The situation improved toward the end of the decade. After the August 1998 default, the Russian economy did begin to turn around. Certain circumstances proved beneficial: the ruble was devalued, domestic production increased and imports were reduced, and the worldwide price of oil rose. However, I also believe that an important factor was a shift away from the pseudo-liberal policies that counted on the "almighty market" to sort things out, to regulate itself, and to stimulate increased production.

Advocates of these policies in Russia relied on recipes provided primarily by U.S. experts who championed their liberal methods but ignored the fact that these methods had never been used by any nation—not even the United States—to recover from a crisis. In their pure form, these methods had not been up to the task since the New Deal. In contrast to the Russian pseudo-liberals, whose slogan was the less government in the economy, the better, captains of the U.S. economy continually tinker and adjust the degree of government involvement (read: interference) in the economy according to changing requirements.

The governmentalists (*gosudarstvenniki*), whose influence increased as the pseudo-liberals fell out of favor, should not be viewed as command economy advocates. The command economy in Russia was utterly defunct: it had blocked the Russian economy from absorbing the fruits of scientific and technological progress; it caused Russia to lag ever further behind the leading industrialized nations; and it fostered the growth of antidemocratic forces in society. There is no real chance we will return down that path. In reality, Russian *gosudarstvenniki* are those who hold statist-liberal views. They fully accept the need for market transformation in our economy and do not diminish the importance of the market as a regulatory force. But they feel the government should use its methods to pursue two goals: first, to establish a civilized market operating on principles of free competition; and second, to shape a socially oriented market economy.

Russia's future economic development depends completely on shifting our economic practices away from the pseudo-liberal approach toward a statist-liberal one. It appears this is taking place in spite of lurching progress and a few appalling lapses. The transformation should make it possible to modernize the economy, achieve high levels of growth in gross domestic product (GDP), and improve our standard of living.

At first glance, it appeared that *official* Washington was not directly responsible for the economic restructuring recommendations that came to us through the Chicago professors, the "Washington Consensus," or the International Monetary Fund (IMF). But this is not so. The U.S. State Department, the Department of the Treasury, and even the White House made it clear to the Russian leaders, in every way possible, that it was necessary to follow and implement this advice. The United States was insistent and stood squarely behind the IMF as it extended to Russia loans determined solely by Moscow's willingness to accept them. I can relate many examples of this from personal experience as prime minister of the Russian Federation.[1] It was particularly painful that IMF representatives knew beforehand what was going to hit us and basically supported a series of bad decisions made in August 1998 by a group of self-styled Russian specialists invested with power and authority.

I do not believe this was done deliberately to put Russia on the skids, although those motives may have existed in the minds of some. The main problem is that the United States and the West as a whole were biased in favor of the pseudo-liberals. These individuals were insiders, trusted and believed. Yet they provided one-sided information about what was happening in Russia. By contrast, the statist-liberals were shunned and dismissed as antiwesterners, their motives suspect.

This erroneous orientation, one might even say disorientation, might have provoked a U.S.-Russian estrangement that could have deepened to become permanent. President Bush's inauguration was accompanied by an onslaught of press commentary to the effect that Russia's role in U.S. foreign policy would be so reduced that Washington would be able to do as it wished in the world without considering Russia's interests.[2] This line dissolved in the wake of September 11, especially because of the support Putin gave to Bush. Whether or not the earlier Bush resurfaces will depend on how well Washington understands Moscow and remains consistent with the policies it follows with us.

While the powers in Moscow are not homogeneous, the president determines the general direction of policy. Putin's hold on policy will gain strength as the people's disappointment with the traditional left and right opposition, and with covert opposition by those close to Putin, grows. The domestic balance of power is reflected in the consistently high public approval ratings Putin receives compared with the ratings received by various opposition leaders. His ratings are good not because what he says and does is beyond criticism; that is not true for any leader. No; the majority of thinking Russians understand that Putin is the best person to lead Russia today. He stands every chance of being reelected for another term.

Putin's ties to the leaders of many countries—the United States and countries in Europe and Asia—have grown and strengthened since September 11. Yet there are reasons to be cautious. The western media give the impression that those who supply information on Russia from inside the country continue to be pseudo-liberals or their ilk.

Today, aid to Russia from the West, the United States in particular, no longer plays a critical role. Our economy is finally following a free market path on its own, and the Russian people continue to embrace democracy more and more strongly. This is where we are headed. We are formulating our own approaches after the disappointment of solutions previously offered from abroad.

This is not to suggest that Russia is becoming isolationist, or that we advocate only our own solutions to the exclusion of those from the West that have occasionally worked. There are areas in which Russia continues to need the West's help: expanding foreign trade and economic contacts, attracting foreign capital investment to Russia, and bringing Russia into the circle of international organizations that make the rules for the world economy.

The first of these needs could be assuaged by the removal of discriminatory restrictions the United States applies to Russia. Among these are the Jackson-Vanik amendment, which denies Russia most-favored-nation status as a U.S. trading partner, restrictions on many U.S. technology exports, and quotas and sanctions that are used occasionally for no apparent reason against Russian goods.

We need to make sure that expansion of the European Union does not damage the economic relationships Russia has with its newest members or with the EU—our largest trading partner—as a whole. The litmus test for the EU's relationship with Russia will almost certainly be how the issue of Kaliningrad is resolved. EU expansion will surround this Russian enclave with EU member states, which will adhere to the Schengen policy permitting free movement within the EU. They will require visas for travel through their territory between Kaliningrad and the other part of Russia. Will there be special conditions established to allow easier access between Kaliningrad and the rest of Russia? Will the current conditions that foster close cooperation between Kaliningrad and Lithuania, Poland, and other European countries be preserved? These issues demand the closest possible scrutiny. Yet rapprochement with the EU is one of the Russian Federation's primary strategic goals.

Cooperative projects that exploit an international labor force will help draw Russia further into the world economy. Russia can offer much, for example, in joint construction projects in aeronautics and space, energy, and many other fields. We do not come to the global economy empty-handed.

The agreement of Putin and Bush to create conditions for the direct involvement of Russian and American business leaders in high-profile projects is significant. Similar cooperative efforts are taking place between Russia and Europe as well. As president of the Russian Federation's Chamber of Trade and Industry, I have become quite involved in this issue. Russian business has come of age and is now ready to engage in the most complex and creative joint operations with its foreign counterparts. What Russian businesses need more than anything else is government—often political—support. When governments negotiate large-scale joint projects, the foreign partner, as a rule, requests that much of the contract work be awarded to its companies. This is natural. To our great misfortune, this has not been the case for us.

It is also imperative that Russia become more involved with the nuts and bolts operation of the global economy. This is why it has become crucial for Russia to join the World Trade Organization (WTO), an issue we must address head on. Having set down the path to a full market economy and becoming increasingly involved in the world economy, Russia would be ill advised to ignore the organization that sets the rules for international markets. WTO members are responsible in one way or another for 90 percent of the world's trade; there is no question but that we should be a member. Yet subordinate issues remain. Under what conditions do we join? What do we need to do to get ready? What do we need to do here at home to make sure that joining the WTO does not knock the wind out of the sails of the many Russian businesses that for myriad reasons are less competitive than they should be?

The WTO issue again sharply contrasts the pseudo-liberals with those who simply combine a liberal approach with government-level regulation. The former politicize Russia's entrance into the WTO, seeking to make it occur absolutely as soon as possible. They use the same logic heard before: first it was shock therapy through price liberalization and privatization, now it is shock therapy by jumping into the WTO. Opponents of this approach favor getting ready before joining, so as to minimize the trauma to Russian businesses. Which of these approaches will the West pin its hopes on? The answer will either facilitate Russia's entrance into the WTO or make it more difficult.

Six Points on Chechnya

Russia's single largest problem today is the situation in Chechnya, which also represents the front line in our own war on terror. By all reckoning, it is time to shift our approach. Our primary strategic goal will not change; Chechnya must remain a part of the Russian Federation. But the time has come to reexamine the tactics we use to reach this goal.

Our previous approach to Chechnya has only partly justified itself. Federal forces have been successful in seriously disrupting the ability of the rebels to organize. This can be credited to the army, to units of the Ministry of Internal Affairs, and most of all to the individual soldiers and officers in the field. Yet the Chechen resistance has not been completely broken, as evidenced by frequent rebel sorties that continue to inflict heavy losses on federal forces. It would not be fair to blame this on the federal command, which is doing its best. The fact is that the problem of Chechnya will not be resolved by purely military means. At this stage it is not primarily a military problem.

Many successful special operations by the Russian Federal Security Service (FSB) have resulted in the removal or capture of several rebel leaders, including such odious individuals as Salman Raduev, Ibn al-Khatab, and others. However, we have not yet been able to destroy the rebels' command structure, and by all accounts they continue to be led from a single command center.

Federal forces have managed to gain the cooperation of several key Chechen leaders. This is not to say that the Chechen problem can be effectively dealt with by the Chechens themselves. The economic infrastructure is below par, embezzlement is widespread, and black market sales of Russian weapons to Chechen rebels continue. Despite the high level of heroism of the federal troops deployed to fight in Chechnya, incidents of abuse and looting by Russian forces do occur from time to time. This is characteristic of any army involved in a protracted, bloody fight against a capable, nimble, strong foe, especially one that has support from a considerable part of the local population.

Chechen rebels, however, have relied on terrorist tactics for the entire course of the fighting. Their goals are to kill as many federal troops as possible, by whatever means; to inflict violent retribution on Chechens who defect from their cause; and to engage in acts such as the taking of hostages (including foreign aid workers), human trafficking, and smuggling to raise funds. Finally, the rebels have undertaken brutal terrorist attacks against civilians living in parts of the Russian Federation outside Chechnya.

What is the proper response to such a situation? I know that the following might draw criticism and even anger from some of those who have been heavily involved in finding a resolution to the problem of Chechnya. But these are my views on the issue, and I feel I have a right and moral obligation to share them.

First, we must do everything possible to isolate the civilian population from the rebels. This is the most important thing we can do at this stage. Unfortunately, we did not accomplish this at the outset of our war on terrorism: the rebels gathered in populated areas, which resulted in heavy civilian casualties during fighting or cleanup operations. Hindsight is twenty-twenty, but losses could have been minimized if efforts to separate the civilian population from the rebels had been made a priority at the start.

As it stands now, we are trying to achieve this separation by allowing local Chechens to have their own government and to maintain their own security forces in populated areas. By itself, this is not proving to make much of a difference; at least, it will not make much of a difference any time soon. There is no reason to believe that the Chechen population is distancing itself from the rebels in any great number, even when the rebels have gone hunting for those inclined to cooperate with the federal troops. Admittedly, local Chechens seem to have more animosity toward than sympathy for the federal authorities there. Any talk about a sea change in this regard is just telling people what they want to hear.

Second, unless we negotiate with at least some of the rebel leaders (those willing to distance themselves from terrorism and to work for reconstruction), our tactic of giving Chechens local administrative authority and responsibility for security will fail.

Elections are not the perfect solution either. In and of themselves, elections would not change anything, even if respectable and talented individuals were entrusted with leadership positions in Chechnya. Chechnya is simply not ready for us to turn the reins over to local authority, as has already been done in other parts of the federation. Local authorities are simply not yet strong enough to immerse themselves in fighting against the rebels after taking on self-governance. And this is a war that can be stopped only through negotiations. Free elections in Chechnya cannot be seen as an alternative to negotiations.

Third, there are some indications that some rebels would be receptive to negotiating and not simply using talks as a ploy to gain time to regroup. Since September 11, Chechen separatists have found it more difficult to receive financial support and to transport mercenaries from international terrorist centers. And certainly they find far less moral support for their cause from abroad than they did before the September 11 attacks. In this respect, the U.S. operation in Afghanistan has had a positive effect. Chechen rebels are no longer using Afghanistan as a base for training and supply. I think both the Saudi and Turkish authorities are going to be keeping a much closer watch on those in their countries who actively support the Chechen separatists. The same is true of Georgia. There are indications that the government there will amend its policies vis-à-vis the Chechen rebels to preserve the interests Georgia shares with Russia. It will not move as far toward this as we would like, but it will make more of an effort.

Let me digress for a moment and address the question of relations between Moscow and Tbilisi. Georgia has done much that Russia has a right to be dissatisfied with. At first, Tbilisi would not acknowledge that Chechen rebels were even located within their territory and refused our suggestion to cooperate in sealing the border Chechen rebels were using to slip into Russia. They refused to hand over known terrorists—Russian citizens—and withheld information about rebel movements near the Russian border. And they also refused our suggestion of joint operations against the terrorists who had established themselves in the Pankisi Gorge. None of these charges is fabricated; the situation cannot help but make Russians angry at the Georgian leaders. We must be clear on this: although the war against the Chechen separatists is significant, it is but one episode in Russia's relationship with Georgia, with which we have historically had friendly relations. Our difficulty with Georgia regarding the Chechen war is not the sum of our relationship, as some have indicated. Fortunately, the situation has somewhat improved, and that makes the future look more optimistic.

But to return to the question of opening up negotiations between the Russian Federation and Chechen separatists: Vladimir Putin's policy after September 11 included the possibility of negotiations between a Putin administration representative and someone to be named by Aslan Maskhadov (the so-called president of Ichkeria, the term used by the separatists to designate an independent Chechen Republic). The initiative was not pursued with vigor and perhaps was even deliberately derailed. Emphasis was not placed on giving the Chechens a seventy-two-hour period in which to announce their willingness to begin negotiating disarmament, although this had been Putin's plan. Instead, the Chechens were given seventy-two hours to disarm, and the result was utterly predictable. Negotiations need to be taken seriously, and not subverted for some ulterior motive. They must be treated as a well-thought-out strategic tool for reaching a solution.

We must plan for a negotiation process that takes place with incremental steps. The goal of our first negotiations must be a cease-fire. We must also insist that before negotiations begin, the Chechen separatist leaders publicly renounce all terrorist acts. If any individual or commander in the negotiating parties cannot meet this requirement and stick with it, continued negotiation will not be possible. We must find Chechen leaders who are ready to meet this requirement.

I would like to stress once again that prospects for talks do not rule out either large-scale decisive military strikes (which would require significant numbers of federal forces to remain in place) or increasing cooperation with those Chechens who have already renounced the war and desire to begin the process of reconstruction.

Fourth, both the events of September 11 and our own experience with terrorism demonstrate how important it is to localize and contain terrorist movements. The regions neighboring Chechnya—especially

Ingushetia, Karachaevo-Cherkessia, and Dagestan—cannot escape their complicity in a situation that allows Chechen rebels to work with local colleagues in these areas to prepare for and carry out terrorist attacks elsewhere on Russian soil. These republics must be viewed as the front line and given appropriate attention, and not only by the federal special services. The invasion of Dagestan by Shamil Basaev in 1999, when local militias fought to contain and repel Chechen armed formations, demonstrates with exceptional clarity that throughout the northern Caucasus there exists a patriotic backbone—a profound loyalty to the Russian Federation—that can substantially assist the war on terrorism by preventing terrorists from crossing the borders from Chechnya. We must use all available federal resources to take administrative, political, economic, and, if necessary, military action to combat the separatist forces in the territories surrounding Chechnya.

The Stavropol region is a special case. The border it shares with Chechnya must be tightly controlled, with the ability to screen all suspicious individuals attempting to cross. This may be a temporary measure, but tight control of this border should be maintained until the end of the Chechen crisis.

Fifth, while the effort of the Russian military has been significant, and military personnel have generally managed to fulfill their roles and remain true to military ideals, it is not up to them to make decisions regarding the continuation of large-scale military operations or ending a stalemate. An example is the Khasavyurt peace agreement signed in 1996, concluding the first war in Chechnya. Each of us has a role to play. It is the job of the politicians to independently develop responsible solutions and then follow through to make sure they are carried out, even by the military. Those who do not defer to authority or who make their own rules must be removed.

A representative of the Russian executive branch should manage everything in Chechnya—reconstruction, military operations against the rebels, and assistance to the local government bodies—to secure the situation. This representative must have authority over the Ministry of Defense, Internal Affairs, and FSS offices in Chechnya, as well as over the local administrative offices. This individual would be responsible for implementing the Russian president's policies for the Chechen republic, which could be designated a special presidential region (*okrug*).

Having all authority in the hands of one individual with direct access to President Putin would avoid inconsistent action, tighten discipline, and increase the accountability for everyone involved in Chechnya. It would also help avert situations where the negligence of the Defense Ministry and Ministry of Interior local commands creates more victims, who otherwise could have been spared, had we learned from our earlier mistakes and not let criminals go unpunished.

The president must be assured of having the best, most up-to-date and current information there is on Chechnya. Years of military operation have provided much falsified and one-sided reporting, frequently resulting in poor analysis and forecasting. This type of behavior must be dealt with harshly. Reports to the leadership in Moscow must be completely honest and unvarnished.

Finally, the events of September 11 can help the rest of the world understand what we are up against in Chechnya. The world must understand once and for all what a heavy burden we are carrying in Chechnya and how trying it has been to fight on this most bloody front in the war against terrorism. Even more so when Russia is so frequently misunderstood. Solidarity against terrorism should be expressed not only by Russian support for the U.S. action in Afghanistan, but by support from the United States, the West, and any other able bodies for our fight against terrorism in Chechnya.

I had formulated these six points prior to the tragic events of October 23, 2002, when Chechen terrorists seized a Moscow theater and took the audience and actors hostage. They held more than eight hundred hostages for three days and lined the theater with explosives. A group of the hostages managed to make contact with REN TV, and I learned from their broadcast that the group was asking that I contact the terrorists. There were already several people negotiating with the hostage takers, trying to secure the release of those being held.

I informed the appropriate government authorities and made my way through the security lines and into the theater. I was accompanied by Ruslan Aushev, former president of Ingushetia, and Aslanbek Aslakhanov, a native Chechen and former general in the Interior Ministry (and currently Chechnya's representative in the Duma). We met with the terrorists' leader, Movsar Baraev, and four other armed terrorists. With the exception of those standing at the door of the room we were in, none of them wore a mask or made any effort to conceal his identity. I was not permitted to enter the hall where the hostages were being held.

The discussion we had with them took an exceptionally harsh tone, which I tried my utmost to avoid. If by taking the hostages the group had wanted to draw attention to the drama in Chechnya and perhaps garner sympathy, they had reached their goal. But the death of the hostages would more than cancel that. Baraev told us, "Attracting attention is just the first step. At noon tomorrow I will start shooting hostages and continue until you withdraw all troops from Chechnya." Attempts to reason with Baraev were cut off when he shouted, "Get out! We're finished talking! I only take orders from Commander Basaev!" I had tried to talk to him about the Chechen respect for the elderly, and the fact that the Quran—to which he had referred—does not condone involving women and children in war. My words had no effect on him, and my requests to take the children out of the theater with me fell on deaf ears.

We were the last negotiators to speak with Baraev, and the theater was stormed by FSB Alpha antiterrorist forces on the night of October 26. Fast-acting gas was introduced into the ventilation system before the operation to immobilize the terrorists, who otherwise would certainly have detonated the explosives and blown up the entire theater. Approximately 700 lives were saved, but 128 of the hostages perished. More than fifty of the terrorists, including Baraev, were killed, and the Alpha forces did not suffer a single casualty.

Was this operation called for? I know for certain that it was, that we had no alternatives. To act any differently would have resulted in losing everyone.

I went to see President Putin immediately after meeting with the terrorists in the theater. He had been completely absorbed with the problem for days, his face ashen from lack of sleep. His only thoughts were how best to save the lives of those hostages. "I have been told by some of those around me," said Putin, "that I should stop the families and relatives from demonstrating and calling for peace in Chechnya. I told them the families could demonstrate in Red Square for all I cared, if it might help save their children and loved ones."

Still, Putin was not in a position to yield to the terrorists' demands. He was speaking for all of Russia.

After these events were over, the issue of negotiating with Chechen field commanders took on a new aspect. Although Aslan Maskhadov had not been directly involved in negotiations up to this point, contact had been maintained with his people. After the October hostage crisis, evidence surfaced suggesting that Maskhadov may have been involved in organizing the terrorist act. Be that as it may, and even if we were to take Basaev at his word that Maskhadov had no knowledge of the attack, it is clear that Maskhadov is not in control of the situation and has no influence with the rebels. If this is the case, then what could negotiations with Maskhadov on the issue of Chechnya possibly yield?

While I remain convinced our strategy must combine military action against rebel bands in Chechnya with negotiations, after the October hostage crisis in Moscow I concluded that it is time to take a break from negotiations. To resume talks, we must find Chechen negotiators that meet two criteria. First, they must be willing to publicly renounce terrorism as a means of reaching their goals; second, they must have some actual influence with the rebels. In addition, we must strengthen the Chechen element among the republic's administrative and legislative bodies before starting to negotiate again.

During the hostage crisis, President Putin was faced with a difficult but clear choice. On the one hand, he could maintain Russia's integrity, in effect preserving Russia as a country. On the other hand, he could capitulate to the terrorists' provocation, demands, and threats of violence against the hostages to begin a negotiation process that ultimately would have led to the same result as the Khasavyurt peace agreement. The Khasavyurt agreement granted Chechnya de facto independence, but this did not lead to peace. Instead, it only caused terrorism and rebel attacks to escalate synergistically.

In March 2003 a referendum held in Chechnya demonstrated that the majority of the population supports the constitution, that is, they believe Chechnya should remain part of the Russian Federation. They also spoke out in favor of a peaceful solution to the present conflict.

Elections for president and a legislative body took place—a significant accomplishment that also changes the situation. I hope that these developments, coupled with amnesty for Chechen rebels not otherwise guilty of criminal activity, can pave the way toward a long-awaited resolution to the problem of Chechnya. At the same time, and despite the significance of what has been achieved, I feel that after two bloody wars it is difficult to pin much hope on lasting peace if it involves establishing a governmental structure in this republic that does not differ in any way from those that already exist in the other eighty-eight parts of the Russian Federation.

Conflicts on Our Borders

In the wake of September 11, more attention must be devoted to resolving the ethnic conflicts that are going on within the territory of the former Soviet Union. Such conflicts are taking an extraordinarily heavy toll on several former Soviet republics. These conflicts are causing problems in the relations of these countries with Russia, and they threaten serious structural damage to the Commonwealth of Independent States (CIS).

The most significant ethnic conflicts currently are the Armenian-Azerbaijani conflict over Nagornyi-Karabakh,[3] the Abkhazian and South Ossetian conflicts in Georgia, and the Trans-Dniestrian conflict in Moldova, all of which have entered their second decade. Each of these started out as an armed confrontation, with actual warfare between the parties. The armed confrontations were brought under control, largely with Russia's assistance. Yet the conflicts continue to simmer, and the parties find themselves physically separated by barricades. Resolution is also more difficult to achieve because the areas created by the fighting—Nagornyi-Karabakh, Abkhazia, Trans-Dniestria, South Ossetia—have become de facto independent entities, indeed, possessing many of the attributes of statehood

At the same time, it is clear that the present situation cannot continue forever in these regions. The conflicts are no longer purely political or military; they are taking an increasingly destructive toll demographically, economically, and in international relations. Here are some examples. The regions of Azerbaijan occupied during the war remain unpopulated;

a significant portion of the Azerbaijan population consists of refugees. The Armenians who occupied these lands have not settled them, nor will they be able to do so. Moreover, the population of Nagornyi-Karabakh—indeed, of Armenia as a whole—is decreasing. By some accounts only 1.5 million people remain in Armenia, most having left for Russia or farther afield.

The persistent nature of the conflict in Abkhazia is largely responsible for Tbilisi's moving politically toward the Chechen separatists. Georgia had originally anticipated that Chechen fighters—who had earlier helped the Abkhazians—might now be helpful on the Georgian side of the conflict. Georgia's use of the Chechen element in the conflict seriously damaged Georgian-Russian relations—a point I have addressed earlier in my remarks on Chechnya.

Tension eased when Georgian special forces went to work in the Pankisi Gorge, taking several rebels into custody and turning them over to the Russian special services. Some saw this as the result of pressure by the United States, which did not want Georgian-Russian relations to boil over.

Although experience shows there is no reason to expect a successful military resolution to the Georgia-Abkhazia conflict, the long years of conflict are pushing some circles in Georgia to try everything but direct military action. For instance, Georgia has frequently insisted on the withdrawal of CIS peacekeeping forces, made up entirely of Russian personnel, from the conflict zone. The Georgians charge that they are not using force to return Georgian refugees to Abkhazia. The arguments that peacekeeping missions must be based on the agreement of both sides regarding their function, and that they differ from missions to "impose peace"—not to mention that peace missions can only be "imposed" with a UN Security Council resolution—fall on deaf ears. At the very last minute, just before the CIS legislative body was to examine the issue of peacekeeping forces in Georgia, Tbilisi extended the force's mandate to operate. Inflammatory tactics like these play into the hands of those who are holding out for a military solution to the problem of Abkhazia. The peacekeeping forces have been successful at keeping the two sides separated and have prevented perilous military escalation more than once. Another full-scale war between Georgia and Abkhazia would have extremely serious consequences for the region.

It is likewise dangerous to allow the current level of conflict in South Ossetia to go unchecked. Refugees from South Ossetia are becoming more and more firmly established in North Ossetia–Alania, a constituent republic of the Russian Federation. Those who support this conflict do so in ignorance of the historically cordial relationship between Georgia and Ossetia.

Both Georgia and Moldova are categorically opposed to granting Abkhazia and Trans-Dniestria, respectively, the right to self-determination through secession. Is there any constructive way to work through this impasse? These conflicts do share certain principles with respect to peace overtures that might be made.

First, there is the principle of territorial integrity. As I mentioned at the beginning of this work, reaffirming the principle of territorial integrity is a sine qua non for helping to stabilize the international system and to reinforce the stability of existing states. During my tenure as Russia's foreign minister, my office worked out a formula that allowed the principle of territorial integrity to be included in a draft agreement between Georgia and Abkhazia. The Foreign Ministry proposed that the sides agree to occupy a common state defined by the borders of the Georgian Soviet Socialist Republic on January 1, 1991 (that is, before the conflict). Based on public opinion among their constituents, the Abkhazian delegation had categorically refused to accept any reference to Georgia's territorial integrity. Nevertheless, through negotiation, we managed to get them to accept our proposal, which amounted to virtually the same thing. Unfortunately, the Georgians balked at signing and insisted that the agreement provide a single constitution that would govern the entire entity. The Abkhazians found it impossible to agree to this.

Despite its ultimate failure, the idea that the two sides might share living space but not one single unified governmental structure seems to me still to be a viable avenue for future negotiations between the Georgians and the Abkhazians, and between the Georgians and South Ossetians. With respect to the Trans-Dniestrian conflict, this arrangement has already been fixed in a document signed by representatives from Moldova and Trans-Dniestria.

A second principle for any peace process needs to be a firm agreement that brings armed combat to an end. Such an agreement should be elevated to the status of a constitutional article, and it would legally establish equality between the warring sides. This is not to say that the two sides would be equal participants in governing a shared state; it is hard to imagine parity in governance of this sort between, for instance, tiny Abkhazia and the entire rest of Georgia, many times larger and more populous. Nevertheless, the signing of such an agreement could relieve the sides of having to adopt a shared constitution at this early stage. Each side in the conflict would have and be governed by its own constitution, the provisions of which should not contradict the agreement to cease armed combat. In other words, a cease-fire settlement could become the foundation for the longer-term construction of an overarching constitutional arrangement.

My third point is to stress the usefulness of federalism as a means of reaching settlements in both Georgia and Moldova. Georgia historically has been subdivided into many regions that differ little from one another ethnically or religiously, for example, Kakhetia, Imeretia, and Guria. Those who oppose a Georgian federation contend that federalism is an attempt to carve the country up into many small pieces. This is not the case; the components of a federation should be given legal status according to certain criteria that unites their area. For example, Abkhazia, South Ossetia, and Adzharia would all be logical federation subjects.[4] The same could be said for Pridnestrovie and Gagauzia in Moldova. A federal structure could be developed for any state, taking into account the considerable expertise and time such a complicated and delicate task would require.

Those involved with the negotiation process frequently encounter the suggestion that a confederacy is what is needed for areas suffering from these conflicts. Practically speaking, however, true confederacies do not exist in the world today. Although nominally a confederacy, Switzerland, for instance, comprises cantons that cannot be considered to have any appreciable sovereignty within the framework of the state that unites them. But federations will differ from one another to the degree that their component federative subjects enjoy independence and attributes of sovereignty.

In March 2003 in Sochi, after negotiations with President Putin, Georgian president Eduard Shevardnadze announced that Georgia would agree to establish a federal structure within Georgia that would grant Abkhazia special status. Abkhazian representatives downplayed this statement and declined the offer. This initial reaction was to be expected, because Russia had suggested the same formula for peace—with agreement from Abkhazia—several times before (including once in 1996 when I was foreign minister). Tbilisi had rejected the offer each time. As the years passed, Abkhazia grew accustomed to the idea of an independent existence, in spite of the obstacles and challenges. Eventually, however, we can expect the two sides to sit down to the negotiating table to hammer out the details of bringing forth a federal structure for Georgia that will grant special status to Abkhazia. There really is no alternative.

To be sure, the principles outlined above are only a starting point. They and other details must be weighed carefully in any specific situation. The main thing is to focus and get started.

And what of the conflict between Armenia and Azerbaijan? From the beginning, one possibility for reaching peace has involved an exchange of territory. Currently, this alternative has become the focus for the high-level negotiations the two sides continue to conduct. In addition to determining the status of Nagornyi-Karabakh and ending the occupation of seven regions in Azerbaijan, negotiations are also addressing the possibility of exchanging Armenian territory for the Lachin Corridor, which connects Nagornyi-Karabakh and Armenia. Negotiators are up against substantial obstacles. The Azerbaijani region of Nakhichevan is an enclave, and Baku is pushing for territorial exchange terms that would join the region with the rest of Azerbaijan. The problem is that Armenia's only border with Iran runs between the two and would be eliminated if they were joined. Erevan wants to retain its direct access to Iran, because the Iranian connection took on great foreign economic significance during Armenia's crisis. The search for a model acceptable to both sides continues.

What the Future Holds

What place will Russia take in the twenty-first century? How will its relationship with the United States and other nations play out? It is difficult to make long-range forecasts, especially when the variables are so numerous. But the dynamics at work in the world today and for the immediate future will establish a great many trends for subsequent years, and some fairly accurate predictions can be made for the beginning of this century.

First, what place will Russia occupy in the world order now taking shape? Its predecessor, the Soviet Union, was a center of power for an extended period of time. The Russian Federation does not rise to the level of the Soviet Union in its might and superpower status. But in any forecasting, it must be remembered that Russia is and will remain the second largest nuclear power in the world. Despite setbacks during the 1990s, the Russian economy and human potential are gaining ground and will be significant forces. Russia's size and natural resources are unparalleled. Its unique position as a bridge between Europe and Asia gives it a more prominent geopolitical role to play in bringing these two civilizations closer together.

That the political commitment and resolve of Russia's leadership today is considerable was demonstrated after September 11. Despite stereotypes to the contrary, Russia was able to maneuver quickly to come out swinging against terrorism and to reinforce overall security. Russia's traditional ties and relationships with many countries and regions of the world will prove useful in the worldwide fight against terror. Despite the serious economic and social problems it faces today, Russia will undoubtedly remain one of the centers of power in a multipolar world.

Second, will Russia be a full-fledged, independent member of the world community? After the end of the cold war the world community—Russia included—was unable to take full advantage of the new environment. When the cold war was waning, euphoria prevailed. The specter of mutually assured destruction had dissipated, and the international community seemed poised to enter a new era of justice and security.

Yet, as Ronald Reagan observed, it takes two to tango. While most Russians eagerly anticipated the dawn of a golden age, looked forward to becoming full members of the world community, and thought they too would be included in helping to build the common European home, many developed countries carried out their policies in a no-holds-barred fashion aimed at pushing their own agenda and national interests to the exclusion of all else. Policy of this kind resulted in Russia's national interests being thwarted, compromised, and squeezed at every turn.

To be sure, the West should not be painted with a broad brush, as there did exist a clash of opinion and a great deal of uncertainty. Under the circumstances, Russia's measured and determined policies could have facilitated a more constructive approach among the western leaders. Development after the cold war might have been less chaotic and more harmonious, but such was not to be. The two former cold war adversaries might have cooperated to work on formulating common policies. Instead, there was a period when Russia seemed to be relegated to taking only a supporting role. As the Russian Federation struggled to establish itself as an independent country after the fall of the USSR, this back-seat stance was advocated by the foreign minister at the time, who expressed it this way: he said the world was divided into the civilized part and the "riff-raff." After losing the cold war, Russia needed to make sure it gained admittance into the club of civilized countries by following their rules. The leader of this club, of course, was the United States.

This approach was not sustainable. This was not because the Foreign Ministry changed leadership, as some in the West have asserted. Dissatisfaction and frustration grew as we tried to play a supporting role to the U.S. lead, while simultaneously coping with the fallout from the end of the cold war. Inside Russia, the majority of people appropriately felt that the end of the cold war did not mean that one of the competing superpowers had been defeated, but that democratic principles had won out over the socialist camp's totalitarian principles. Within a short time the euphoria at democracy's victory in Russia died down, a condition largely ignored by western leaders. This was because Russian democrats were encountering social and economic setbacks that compromised their leadership. In addition, U.S. policies toward Russia, while not altogether hostile to Russia, were also devoid of anything approaching a spirit of partnership. So the second conclusion is that it is not appropriate for Russia to be relegated to playing a supporting role in world events.

This leads, then, to a third question: if Russia is unwilling to play a subordinate role to the United States, will this result in continuing tension between Russia and the United States? I think not—but only if Washington fully grasps how futile and counterproductive it is to try to turn Russia into a vassal subservient to U.S. policy and will. I dare say not one Russian leader would last long in power if he took this approach.

This is not to detract from a closer partnership, which September 11 helped to facilitate, between Russia and the United States. The terrorist attacks led to many new initiatives and opportunities in Russian foreign policy, including discrediting once and for all the notion that Russian-American relations must be conducted according to a zero-sum approach and instead seeking common interests and pursuing those interests with unadulterated cooperation. So, we can conclude that while Russia will not accept subordination to the United States, genuine partnership between the two countries based on shared interests is not only possible but desirable.

Finally, how stable is the trend toward rapprochement between the United States and Russia? Western analysts base their answer to this question on the presence or absence in the Putin administration of serious opposition to his policies, on his commitment to and stamina for maintaining these policies, and, more generally, on the power balance of factions within Russia. I believe that all this is dependent, to a considerable extent, on U.S. policies.

The U.S. unilateral action in Iraq, opposed by the UN, evoked a uniformly negative response with Russians. Even the media outlets that purport to be pro-American and prowestern took an extremely negative position on the war in Iraq. This is a reliable indicator, since they could not afford to ignore the sentiment of the overwhelming majority of Russian citizens. There were even calls for Russia to begin distancing itself from the United States, to pull back from the close relationship that had formed after the September 11 attacks. But this extreme negative reaction was not reflected in the political realm. The foreign policy course charted by President Putin after September 11 remained largely unchanged. One might imagine it could have turned out differently:

—if the threat posed by international terrorism to the entire world did not exist. The United States is an essential party in the effective fight against international terrorism and in efforts to resolve the international and ethnic conflicts that foster it.

—if the world believed that the U.S.-led war truly represented an irreversible rejection of the joint policies developed to help stabilize various parts of the world in conflict. Some politically influential circles in the United States do not wish to pay for unilateral decisions with large losses of life, with the loss of important allies, or with growing isolation of the United States.

—if the world had returned to a cold war mentality. In a non–cold war environment, playing a strongly anti-American hand could land Russia into serious international hot water. Such a stance could drive those European powers who presently act with some independence, indeed the EU as a whole, into the arms of the United States, while at the same time attracting to Russia more destructive forces. All of this would substantially weaken Russia's international role.

—if we were not completely sure that the overall course of global development would compensate for any irregularity or inconsistency in U.S. policy.

Russia's decision not to break off its partnership with the United States does not mean Russia is ready to aid and abet the United States in decisions and actions where it is mistaken. On the contrary, developing relations with the United States puts Russia in a much better position to exert a positive influence on U.S. policy.

After the U.S. war against Iraq, Russia must concentrate on finding solutions to its own vexing domestic problems and building up its military strength. It is important to determine whether or not Russian-U.S. rapprochement has room to allow Russia to pursue, as it must, a diversified foreign policy. Will we be able to develop relations with the EU or bilateral ties with the nations of Europe, with China, India, Japan, the Arab world, Latin America, or Africa? One should not preclude the other. And the United States must not view Russian foreign policy initiatives in other directions as running counter to rapprochement with the United States.

Among Americans, the idea is spreading that those countries that rallied around the United States after September 11 are bound to adhere to views and principles identical to those of the United States. This applies to both strategic principles and tactical principles, some of which have nothing whatsoever to do with the war on terrorism. Moreover, the United States seems to believe in the absolute truth of its views in all matters and to expect its antiterrorism partners to conform to U.S. views on a wide range of vital issues.

Russia's desire to play an active role in the global community should not be misinterpreted. Russia's desire to keep its status as a great world power has absolutely nothing to do with aspirations for empire building, a motive that is occasionally attributed to us. Rather, this desire stems from our knowledge that Russian foreign policy can do much to help stabilize conflict situations in regions around the world. Russia is certainly as interested in this as any other nation of the world, perhaps more so. Moreover, isolation from the world community can only harm Russia and its efforts to resolve the economic, social, and political issues it faces.

Russia will almost certainly not pull back from the rapprochement that has been achieved with the United States since 9/11, but whether the relationship deepens and strengthens now depends largely on Washington.

Afterword

If the United States works toward creating a viable, multipolar world; if it ceases to think itself capable of and responsible for unilaterally resolving critical issues of international stability and security; and if it stops trying to set unilateral rules of conduct for the international community, then Russia can be a true and loyal partner to the United States. The relationship we have developed with the United States since September 11 gives rise to optimism. For the time being, however, this optimism is tempered with caution.

Notes

Chapter One

1. I wrote in detail about this in "Gody v bol'shoi politike" (Years in big policy) (Moscow: Sovershenno sekretno, 2000).

2. *The Guardian,* June 11, 2002.

3. Yossef Bodansky, *Taliby, mezhdunarodnyi terrorizm i chelovek, ob'yavivshiy voinu Amerike* (Moscow: Veche, 2002), p. 271. Originally published in English as *Bin Laden: The Man Who Declared War on America* (Roseville, Calif.: Prima Publishing, 2001).

4. According to the U.S. press, al-Muhajir was an American citizen who traveled extensively to Pakistan and Afghanistan, where he had contact with al Qaeda operatives. If nothing else, this is a clear indication of how extensive a terrorist network can be.

5. G. I. Morozov, *Terrorizm—prestuplenie protiv chelovechestva* (Terrorism—the crime against mankind)(Moscow, 2001), p. 49.

Chapter Two

1. This theory was first published by Huntington in 1993. His book *The Clash of Civilizations and the Remaking of World Order* was translated into Russian and published in Moscow in 1997.

2. In his book *Sud'ba tsivilizatsii. Put'razuma.* (Moscow, 1998), Russian scholar N. N. Moiseev writes: "Toynbee is hardly correct in

asserting that religion gives rise to civilization. [Samuel Huntington also holds this and similar viewpoints.] After all, civilization is older than any religion, and it seems to me rather that the opposite must hold—that civilizations choose their religions and mold them to fit their traditions based on historical experiences. I believe that the characteristics of a particular civilization are determined above all by living conditions, by geography, and by climate" (p. 42). Accepting Moiseev's argument, we must add that religions are an integral part of civilization, and that they truly exert an enormous influence on civilization.

3. All excerpts and quotations are from M. H. Shakir's translation of the Holy Quran, as published by Tahrike Tarsile Quran, Inc., Elmhurst, New York. Passages are identified by number (*sura*) and verse.

4. A. I. Agronomov, *Dzhikhad: "svyashchennaya voina" Mukhammedan* (Moscow: Kraft+, 2002), p. 97.

5. Henri Massé, *Islam* (translated from French) (New York: G. P. Putnam's Sons, 1938), p. 78.

6. Ibid., p. 55.

7. E. A. Beliaev, *Arabs, Islam and the Arab Caliphate in the Early Middle Ages*, translated from the Russian by Adolphe Gourevitch (New York: Praeger, 1969), p. 140.

8. Ray Takeyh, "Faith-Based Initiatives," *Foreign Policy*, vol. 127 (November/ December 2001), p. 70.

Chapter Three

1. Mohamed Hassanein Heikal, *Autumn of Fury: The Assassination of Sadat* (London: Andre Deutsch, 1983), p. 67.

2. Henry Kissinger, *Years of Upheaval* (Boston: Little, Brown, 1982), p. 747.

3. Beginning in the 1960s, the Dartmouth conferences were held alternately in the United States and the USSR. Influential American and Soviet citizens joined together in these meetings to discuss U.S.-Soviet relations.

4. Menachem Begin became prime minister of Israel on June 20, 1977, after his Likud Party won the May elections. He resigned on September 15, 1983. Ezer Weizman, *The Battle for Peace* (Toronto: Bantam, 1981), p. 190.

5. *The Times*, August 30, 1982.

6. *Middle East International*, September 3, 1982, p. 6.

7. *Vremya MN*, February 26, 2003, p. 7.

8. Amin al-Hindi, chief of the Palestinian General Intelligence Agency, reported that Palestinian security forces would not be able to fulfill their mission if Israel did not release the hundreds of agents it had arrested in the West Bank and Gaza.

9. Brent Scowcroft, "Building a Coalition Is the Way to Win This War," *International Herald Tribune*, October 17, 2001.

10. *Financial Times*, October 31, 2001.

11. Edward Bannerman and others, *Europe after September 11th* (London: Centre for European Reform, 2002), p. 23.

Chapter Four

1. *Business Week*, European edition, May 27, 2002, p. 42.

2. Benazir Bhutto, interview with London correspondent of *Argumenty i fakty*, October 10, 2001.

3. Ibid.

Chapter Five

1. The United States has started to fight back, trying to rid itself of dependency on OPEC oil by obtaining what it needs from non-OPEC nations. The United States has also taken stronger steps to break up OPEC. These attempts succeeded somewhat with Libya, which, as compensation for its part in the Lockerbie bombing, threw open its oil production to U.S. cooperation. The foreign media have predicted that Libya will replace Saudi Arabia as the world's primary oil exporter, since the Saudi kingdom has recently been a disappointment to the United States. There is little likelihood of this happening in the near future since Europe and Japan are strongly averse to any destabilization, however fleeting, in the world oil market.

2. Joint Declaration on European Defence. British-French summit, Saint Malo, December 3–4, 1998.

3. *Financial Times*, December 7, 1998.

4. *Vestnik Evropy*, vol. 4 (2002), p. 46.

5. A. A. Kokoshin, V. A. Veselov, and A. V. Liss, *Sderzhivanie vo vtorom iadernom veke* (Moscow: Institute of International Security Problems, Russian Academy of Sciences, 2001), p. 47.

6. Samuel Huntington, *The Clash of Civilizations and the Remaking of World Order*.

Chapter Six

1. *Newsweek*, September 19, 2001.

2. The report of the Commission to Assess United States National Security Space Management and Organization was published on January 11, 2001.

Chapter Seven

1. See *Vosem' mesyatsev plyus* . . . (Eight months plus . . .) (Moscow: Mysl, 2001).

2. "Russia Is Finished" was the title of an article in the May 2001 issue of the *Atlantic Monthly*, and it reflects a sentiment that was shared by many in the Washington establishment.

3. Calling this the "Armenian-Azerbaijani" conflict is in no way intended to downplay the role of Nagorno-Karabakh itself in the origin and rise of this conflict, or in the current peace process.

4. Adzharia was the only Soviet autonomous republic established along religious lines; the Adzhars are ethnically Georgian but practice Islam.

INDEX

Abbas, Mahmoud (Abu Mazen), 42

Abdallah, crown prince of Saudi Arabia, 27, 47

Abdallah, king of Jordan, 87

Abd al-Wahhab, Muhammad ibn, 27

Abkhazia: conflict with Georgia, 126, 127–30

Abu Nidal terrorist organization, 4

Afghanistan: antiterrorist operations in, 76–82; bin Laden in, 12; Caspian Sea oil and gas through, 74; Chechen separatists and U.S. action in, 120; Chechen terrorists in, 4; Iran's support of U.S. actions in, 6; U.S. response to Soviet invasion of, 9; U.S. Stinger missiles for mujahidin, 11. *See also* Karzai, Hamid; Northern Alliance

Aga Khan, 77

Albanian separatists, 13, 22

Albright, Madeleine, 5–6; Clinton's Middle East peace efforts and, 40; on NMD developments, 108; Primakov and, 17; on Russia's promises to Saddam Hussein, 84; on Saint Malo declaration, 100

Alexander I, king of Yugoslavia, 2

Alexander II, tsar of Russia, 2

Allon, Yigal, 45

al Qaeda, 4; achievements, 8; bin Laden's son as head of, 79; desire for WMD, 15; Maktab al-Khidamat, 10–11; range of terrorist activities, 11; Russian support for U.S. strikes against, 67–69; Taliban and, 12–13, 80; U.S. questioning captured members of, 7–8

Annan, Kofi, 51–52, 62–63, 87, 89

Anti-Ballistic Missile (ABM) Treaty, 65, 67, 107, 109, 110

Antimissile systems, 105

Arab-Israeli conflict, 30, 31–32, 103; war of *1973,* 35

Arab League, 42, 83, 92; Follow-up Committee, 57

Arafat, Yassir: meeting with Clinton, 41; meeting with Peres, 42; Mitchell and Tenet peace plans and, 48; Putin's

talks with, 51; Sharon on, 46;
Sharon's hatred of, 44, 53–54;
Sharon surrounds Ramallah bunker
of, 52

Armenia: conflict with Azerbaijan, 126,
127, 130–31

Asharq al-Awsat, 50

Ashcroft, John, 15–16

Aslakhanov, Aslanbek, 124

Assad, Bashir al-, 49, 51

Assad, Hafiz al-, 29, 38, 39

Aum Shinrikyo terrorist network, 3

Aushev, Ruslan, 124

Azerbaijan: conflict with Armenia, 126,
127, 130; rights to Caspian Sea
floor, 75

Azimov, Rustam, 71

Aziz, Tariq, 91–92

Bajpai, Kanti, 76

Bali: terrorist attacks, 2

Ball, George, 43

Baraev, Movsar, 124

Barak, Ehud, 39, 40, 41, 51

Barthou, Louis, 2

Basaev, Shamil, 14, 122, 125

Basque separatists, 2, 3, 66

Begin, Menachim, 37, 43

Beilin, Yossi, 42

Belgium: on Iraq conflict, 90

Belyaev, Evgeny, 25

Ben-Ami, Shlomo, 58

Ben-Eliezer, Benjamin, 54

Berlusconi, Silvio, 31

Bhutto, Benazir, 13, 76, 81

bin Laden, Mohammed Awad, 10

bin Laden, Osama, 4, 7; elusiveness, 76;
events shaping life of, 9–10; German
intelligence on hiding place of, 79;
Russian support for U.S. strikes
against, 67–69; Saudi Arabia and,
11–12; as Uncle Sam in *New York*

Times, 88–89; U.S. actions against
Afghanistan and, 10–11; U.S. intelligence on, 8; on weapons acquisition,
15. *See also* al Qaeda

BinLaden Group, 10

Blair, Tony, 20, 51, 87, 91

Blanco, Luis Carrero, 2

Blix, Hans, 87, 89–90

Bodansky, Yossef, 14

Brzezinski, Zbigniew, 36

Bush, George W.: on cooperative business projects with Russia, 117; Iran
policies, 6, 64; Middle East peace
plan, 47, 54–55; orders military
action in Iraq, 90–91; response to
Massoud's murder, 77; Russia's role
in U.S. foreign policy and, 115; unilateral actions on security, 65; on
U.S. military presence in Europe, 98;
visits mosque after September 11
attacks, 20; on war on terrorism, 93

Bush administration, 74, 83

Bushehr: nuclear power plant construction, 17

Business Week, 74–75

Butler, Richard, 52, 84, 85, 86

Byrd, Robert, 83

Camp David Accord, 37

Carter, Jimmy, 36

Caspian oil reserves, 73–74

Central Asian leaders, 71–72, 73, 75

Central Intelligence Agency (CIA), 11,
110

Chechnya: amnesty for noncriminal
separatists, 126; bin Laden and
Chechen separatists, 12, 14;
Georgian-Russian relations and,
127; isolating civilians from rebels
in, 119; negotiations with rebel
leaders, 119–20, 121, 124–25;
referendum on constitution in, 126;

self-determination for, 22; solving
Russian problem in, 118–19; ter-
rorists, 3–4, 77, 119–23. *See also*
Moscow hostages
Chemical, biological, radiological, and
nuclear (CBRN) agents, 15
China: alliance with India and Russia,
75–76; economic importance, 95;
on Iraq conflict, 89; neutralizing
Afghan terrorists and, 82; U.S.
antiterrorist operation in
Afghanistan and, 70–71; U.S.
influence on, 95
Chirac, Jacques, 51, 89
Christians: in Arab nations, 25–26; in
the Quran, 27
Clinton, Bill, 16–17, 39–40, 41, 51, 84
Cold war, 94; Arab-Israeli conflict and,
32–33; as model of international
relations, 20; space-based nuclear
tests during, 106–07; UN and, 60
Commonwealth of Independent States
(CIS), 72–73, 75
Communications: globalization of,
96–97
Comprehensive Test Ban treaty (*1963*),
110
Cook, Robin, 91
Cultural diversity, 22, 24, 105

Dagestan, 122
Dayan, Moshe, 37
"Declaration on the Strategic Partner-
ship and Cooperation Framework
between the Republic of Uzbekistan
and the United States," 71
De Michelis, Gianni, 53
Democracy vs. terrorism, 103
al-Dora: biological agent research and
development, 83
Drug trade, 12, 13, 79
Durand Line, 79

Egypt: adoption of Islam in, 25; Islamic
extremists in, 3, 28; Middle East
Quartet proposals, 56–57. Israeli
peace treaty (*1979*) with, 37; Jordanian initiative with, 49; *See also*
Mubarak, Hosni; Sadat, Anwar
Ekeus, Rolf, 84
Energy resources market: U.S. presence
in Central Asia and, 76
Ethnic groups: conflict escalation, 103;
conflicts in former Soviet Union,
126–27; end to armed combat by,
129; federalism and, 129–30; territorial integrity and self-determination,
128–29
Eurasian economic community, 72
European Bank for Reconstruction and
Development, 49–50
European Union: Arab protests at
Sharon's Arafat policy and, 52; economic importance, 95; Iran's terrorism policies and, 5; on Iraq conflict,
91; Middle East Quartet and, 55;
military and political component of,
99–100; neutralizing Afghan terrorists and, 82; Palestinian-Israeli talks
in Taba and, 42; Russia's concerns
about expansion of, 116–17; Sharm
el-Sheikh summit and, 40; terrorism
policies of, 4; U.S. support for NATO
expansion and, 98–99
Everts, Steven, 58
Extradition agreements, 18–19

al-Fallujah: chemical weapons produc-
tion, 83
Farouk, king of Egypt, 28
Federal Bureau of Investigation (FBI),
7–8
Former Soviet Union: rise of Islamic
fundamentalism in, 29. *See also*
Union of Soviet Socialist Republics

Framework for Peace in the Middle East, 37
France, 89, 90, 91. *See also* Chirac, Jacques
Fraser, Malcolm, 61, 63
Fundamentalism, extremism vs., 27–30

Gandhi, Indira, 3
Georgia: Abkhazian and South Ossetian conflicts with, 126, 127–30; Chechen separatists and, 120; Russia's relations with, 73, 120–21; U.S. and oil pipeline through, 74; U.S. military deployments in, 69–70; and U.S. relations with Central Asian leaders, 71
Germany, 89, 90, 91, 97. *See also* Schmidt, Helmut; Schroeder, Gerhard
Globalization, 15, 29, 96, 97
Gody v bolshoi politike (Primakov), 84
Gore, Al, 17, 40, 62, 88
Great Britain, 59, 66, 87. *See also* Blair, Tony
Gryadunov, Yu. S., 45
Gush Emunim group, 43

Al-Hamad Al-Sabah, Jaber Mubarak, 88
Hamadi, Sa'adon, 92
Hamas, 11
Haq, Abdul, 78
Hebron protocol of *1997,* 54
Heikal, Mohamed Hassanein, 34–35, 49
Helsinki negotiations on NMD developments *(1997),* 108
Hezbollah, 6
Hijackings: by PFLP, 45
Humanitarian intervention, 59; definition of, 63; international terrorism and, 66; UN mechanism vs., 63–64
Human rights, 104

Huntington, Samuel, 20–21, 101
Hussein, Saddam, 82, 83, 84, 91–92

Ibn al-Kahtab, 118
India: alliance with China and Russia, 75–76; neutralizing Afghan terrorists and, 82; nuclear weapons and Pakistan conflict, 16–17, 111; U.S. influence on, 95
Ingushetia, 122
Integration, economic, 97
Intelligence agencies, 6–9, 103
InterAction Council, 65–66
Intermediate Range Nuclear Forces (INF) Treaty, 109
International Atomic Energy Commission (IAEA), 17, 111
International Monetary Fund (IMF), 114–15
International relations: competition between civilizations, 20–21; need for united counterforce against terrorism, 104; Russia's world role, 113, 132–35; September *11* attacks and, 102
Internet: Muslim society and, 29
Iran: Armenian-Azerbaijani conflict and, 131; bin Laden and, 12; Iraq and, 83; neutralizing Afghan terrorists and, 82; nuclear problems in, 17, 18; terrorism policies, 4, 5–6; U.S. antiterrorist operation in Afghanistan and, 70–71; U.S. influence on, 95; as U.S. target, 92–93
Iraq: bin Laden and, 12; Russian opposition to U.S. action in, 133–34; Sharon's encouragement of U.S. action, 46; UN weapons inspections in, 84, 85, 89–90; U.S. action in, 82–83, 92; use of force against without UN sanction, 59, 61

Iraqi Atomic Energy Commission, 83
Irish Republican Army, 2–3
Islam: fundamentalism vs. extremism, 27–30; modernization, 29; spread of, 24–25; sentiments on aggressiveness, 20; violence of, 26. *See also* Muslims; Quran
Islamic extremists, 3, 9, 24, 30. *See also* Muslim reactionary groups
Islamic Movement of Uzbekistan (IMU), 73
Israel: Arab-Israeli conflict and, 32–33; creation of, 57; nuclear weapons and, 111. *See also* Middle East peace process
Ivanov, Ivan, 51
Ivanov, Sergei, 88

Jackson-Vanik amendment, 116
Japan, 95, 97
Jerusalem, 26, 58
Jewish extremists, 3
Jews: in Arab nations, 25–26; in the Quran, 27
Jordan, 56–57, 83, 88

Kaliningrad, 116–17
Kalyaev, Ivan, 2
Karachaevo-Cherkessia, 122
Karimov, Islam, 71
Karzai, Hamid, 74, 77, 78
Kazakhstan, 72, 75
Kennedy, John F., 2
Khaksar, Mohammed, 12–13
Khalilzad, Zalmay, 74
Khasavyurt peace agreement, 122, 125
Khatami, Mohammed, 5
Khattab, Ibn al, 14
Kissinger, Henry, 34–35
Kokoshin, A. A., 100
Kosovo, 22, 62

Kosovo Liberation Army, 13, 62
Kuwait, 83, 88
Kyrgyzstan, 69, 70, 71

Lebanese Christian Phalangist militia, 43–44
Lebanon, 25, 43, 56–57, 83
Libya, 4–5
Likud Party, Israel, 38, 39, 42–43
Liss, A. V., 100
Lockerbie bombing, 5

Macedonia: Albanian separatism in, 62
Madrid Peace Conference *(1991)*, 34, 37–38, 39–42
Maktab al-Khidamat (MAK), 10–11. *See also* al Qaeda
Marchese, George, 13
Maskhadov, Aslan, 121, 124–25
Massé, Henri, 25
Massoud, Ahmad Shah, 77
McIllwain, J. Peter, 13
Middle East conflict. *See* Arab-Israeli conflict
Middle East peace process: Clinton's peace efforts and, 39–40; cold war and, 32–34; duration of, 32; Egypt-Israel peace treaty, 37; land-for-peace formula, 34; Madrid Peace Conference *(1991)* and, 38; Middle East Quartet proposals and, 56, 57; Mitchell and Tenet plans, 48–49; post–September *11*, 31–32; Primakov plan, 50; two-pronged approach by U.S., 34–38
Mitchell, George, 48–49
Moldova, 126, 129–30
Moratinos, Miguel, 42
Morozov, G. I., 18
Moscow theater hostages, 2, 123–24
Mountbatten, Louis, 2

Moussa, Amre, 49
Mubarak, Hosni, 49, 51
Muhajir, Abdullah al-, 15–16
Muhammad, 23, 26
Multipolarity, 95–98, 100–01
Musharraf, Pervez, 77, 80
Muslim Brotherhood, 3, 28–29
Muslims, 19, 21. *See also* Islam; Quran
Muttahida Majlis-e-Amal (MMA), 79

Nagornyi-Karabakh, 126, 127, 130
Najibullah, Mohammed, 81
Namangani (Khodjiev), Juma, 73
Nasser, Gamal Abdel, 28
National missile defense (NMD) systems, 100, 107–08
NATO, 9, 62, 64, 91, 98; NATO-Russia Council, 64–65
Nazarbaev, Nursultan, 72
Netanyahu, Benjamin, 39
NMD. *See* National missile defense systems
Noor, queen of Jordan, 52
Northern Alliance, 12, 69, 77–78
North Korea, U.S. influence on, 95
North-South relationships, 103–05
Nuclear nonproliferation, 105; ABM treaty and, 109–10; alternatives strategies for, 111; intelligence agencies on, 110; UN Security Council membership and, 111–12
Nuclear Non-Proliferation Treaty (NPT, *1968*), 17, 110
Nuclear power, 16, 17–18, 111
Nuclear weapons, 14, 15–16, 60, 95. *See also* Weapons of mass destruction
Nussibeh, Sari, 58

Omar, Khalif, 25
Omar, Mohammed, 12

Operation Desert Fox, 86
Organization for Security and Cooperation in Europe (OSCE), 98
Organization of Petroleum Exporting Countries (OPEC), 74, 95–96
Oslo negotiations on Middle East peace, 34, 38, 44, 47
Ottomans, 28
Outer Space Treaty (*1967*), 107, 109
Owen, David, 100

Padilla, Jose, 15–16
Pakistan: Afghan terrorists and, 82; anti-Taliban sentiment in, 77; Inter-Services Intelligence Agency, 79–80; nuclear weapons and India conflict, 16–17, 111; Pashtun tribal regions in, 79; Taliban and, 16; U.S. enlists antiterrorism support from, 53; U.S. influence on, 95
Palestine Liberation Organization (PLO), 28; Clinton's Middle East efforts and, 40; Clinton's peace plan and, 41–42; Hamas and, 11; Madrid Peace Conference and, 38; relocates from Lebanon to Tunis, 44. *See also* Arafat, Yassir
Palestinian Authority, 6, 46, 57
Palestinian Islamic Jihad, 4, 28
Palestinian state: Ad Hoc Liaison Committee on economic development for, 55–56; Bush plan on, 54–55; Middle East Quartet on, 55; Sharon on, 45–46; UN Security Council resolution on, 52
Palestinian terrorists, 43
Pashtun tribes, 77–78, 79
Peres, Shimon, 38, 39, 42, 47, 51
Perovskaya, Sophia, 2
Popular Front for the Liberation of Palestine (PFLP), 4, 45

Poverty, international terrorism growth and, 103–04

Powell, Colin, 51, 52–53

Primakov, Yevgeny M.: Albright and, 5; Arab state visits *2001*, 49; delivers message from Putin to Hussein, 91–92; De Michelis and, 53; Libyan diplomacy, 4–5; Middle East peace plan, 50–51; Middle East talks, 36; Moscow hostages and, 123–24; PFLP airplane hijackings and, 45; on response to Chechen terrorists, 119–23; as foreign minister, 39

"Principles of Islamic Law Concerning the War against Infidels," 24

Putin, Vladimir, 31; Arafat meets with, 41; calls Arafat in Ramallah, 52; calls Bush on Massoud's murder, 76–77; on cooperative business projects with U.S., 117; on Iraq conflict, 90; Middle East deadlock and, 51; military reports on Chechnya to, 123; negotiations with Chechen separatists, 121, 124–25; Peres's discussion with, 51, 52; Russian economic reforms and, 115; Russian–U.S. relations, 133–34; Shevardnadze and, 130; support for U.S. war on terrorism, 68–69, 70

Qadaffi, Muammar, 4

Qadi, Haji Abdul, 78

Quandt, William, 36

Quran, 23; Palestinian territory and, 26–27; tenets of, 24, 124; Wahhabism and, 27. *See also* Islam

Rabin, Yitzhak, 3

Radioactive dirty bombs, 15–16

Raduev, Salman, 118

Reagan, Ronald, 132

Red Brigades, 3

Religious tolerance of nonbelievers, 25, 105

Rice, Condoleezza, 8

Ritter, Scott, 84

Ross, Dennis, 50

Rumsfeld, Donald, 16, 70, 107

Russian Federation: on ABM treaty, 110; alliance with India and China, 75–76; Chamber of Trade and Industry, 117; Chechen terrorists, 3–4; on collective development of antimissile systems, 108; collective security among Shanghai Six, 75; command economy, 114; cultural-religious world division and, 21; economic reforms, 113–15, 131; on European expansion, 116–17; executive oversight in Chechnya by, 122–23; Federal Security Service, 118, 124; Foreign Intelligence Service, 6–7, 9, 110; Georgia's relations with, 120–21; Georgia's territorial integrity and, 71–72; Iran's terrorism policies and, 5; on Iraq and weapons monitoring, 87; on Iraq conflict, 90, 91, 133–34; Jackson-Vanik amendment, 116; Madrid Peace Conference and, 37–38; Middle East deadlock and, 51; Middle East Quartet and, 55; neutralizing Afghan terrorists and, 82; nineteenth-century terrorism in, 2; on NMD developments, 108; nuclear nonproliferation and, 17; as nuclear power, 131; on preservation of UN mechanism, 63; prospects, 131–35; response to September *11* attacks, 131–32; Sharm el-Sheikh summit, 40; terrorism concerns after September *11*, 121–22, 123; terrorism policies, 4;

on terrorist actions in Middle East, 44–45; on UN inspectors in Iraq, 89; UNSCOM weapons inspections in Iraq and, 84–85, 86; U.S. unilateral security actions, 65; world role, 113, 131–35

Sadat, Anwar, 3, 33, 34–35
Saint Malo declaration, 99–100
Saltanov, Alexander, 87
Sarin gas, 3
Saudi Arabia: bin Laden and, 11–12; Chechen separatists and, 120; democratization of Islam in, 29; headquarters of bin Laden Group, 10; Iraq and, 83; on Iraq conflict, 88; Middle East Quartet proposals and, 56, 57; Wahhabism in, 28
Schmidt, Helmut, 65
Schroeder, Gerhard, 51, 89
Scowcroft, Brent, 53, 58
Sedney, David, 7
Separatism: Islamic extremists and, 30; territorial integrity and, 21–22, 128–29
September 11, 2001, terrorist attacks, 1–2; anti-Muslim sentiment following, 20; international relations and, 102; lessons, 103; Middle East peace process and, 32; nuclear nonproliferation after, 111; preparations for, 7; Russia-U.S. relations after, 133; Russia's concerns about Chechen terrorists after, 121–22, 123; U.S. Middle East policy after, 53
Sergei Alexandrovich, grand duke, 2
Shanghai Cooperation Organization (SCO, Shanghai Six), 75
Sharaa, Farouk al-, 38
Sharm el-Sheikh summit meetings, 40–41, 51

Sharon, Ariel: hard line against Palestinians, 42–43, 45; January 2003 elections and, 57; Mitchell and Tenet peace plan and, 48; murders of Palestinians and, 43–44; on Palestinian state, 45–46; personal action against Arafat by, 52, 53–54; Sharm el-Sheikh summit and, 40–41
Shevardnadze, Eduard, 130
Shultz, George, 45
Sikh separatists, 3
South Ossetia: conflict with Georgia, 126, 128, 129–31
Space: alternatives to militarism, 108–09; cold war nuclear tests, 106–07; militarism of, 105–06; Outer Space Treaty, 107, 109; space-based interceptors, 108; U.S. dominance of, 76
Space Commission, 107
Spain: Basque separatists, 66
Sponeck, Hans von, 82–83
Stavropol region, 122
Strategic Arms Limitation Talks (SALT I and II), 107, 108, 109
Sudan: bin Laden and, 12
Suicide: suicide bombers, 31, 51, 54; Quran prohibition of, 24
Superpowers: definition of, 94–95; multipolar vs. unipolar, 95–96; nuclear weapons and, 14
Syria, 38–39, 57, 83, 92–93

Taba: Palestinian-Israel discussions in, 42
Tajikistan, 69
Takeyh, Ray, 30
Talbott, Strobe, 17
Taliban: bin Laden and, 12; centers of, 78–79; Chechen rebels and, 77; fighting capabilities, 81; in Karzai's

government, 80; Pakistan and, 16, 79–80; partisan raids in Afghanistan by, 79; U.S. aid in formation of, 13

Tenet, George, 8, 48–49

Territorial integrity, 21–22, 128–29

Terrorism: as criminal vs. political act, 18; charter against terrorism proposed, 18; as deterrent against terrorism, 44; global, 3, 31, 59, 66; U.S. war on, 59, 65–66, 93

Terrorist groups: extradition of, 18–19; global information sharing on, 8–9; infrastructure in Afghanistan, 13–14; nationalistic, 4–6; non-state-aligned, 6–7, 14. *See also* al Qaeda

Towards Peace in the Middle East, 36

Trans-Dniestrian conflict in Moldova, 126, 128, 129

Transnationalism, economic, 97

Treaty Banning Nuclear Weapon Tests in the Atmosphere, in Outer Space and Under Water (*1963*), 107

Trepov, Dmitry, 2

Tucker, Jonathan, 83

Turkey, 83, 88, 120

Union of Soviet Socialist Republics: aircraft hijackings and, 45; cold war and, 14; joint statement on Middle East peace, 37; Kissinger in Middle East peace process and, 35; Madrid Peace Conference and, 37–38; Middle East peace process and, 33, 34; on terrorist actions in Middle East, 44–45. *See also* Former Soviet Union

United Nations: code of conduct for new world order, 104; humanitarian interventions and, 63–64; Middle East Quartet and, 55; NATO intervention in Yugoslavia and, 62–63;

neutralizing Afghan terrorists and, 82; right to use force under, 60–61; self-determination and, 21; WWII and, 60. *See also* Annan, Kofi; United Nations Security Council

United Nations Monitoring, Verification and Inspection Commission (UNMOVIC), 87, 89–90

United Nations Security Council: Arab-Israeli conflict resolutions, 32; on Iraq and weapons monitoring, 85, 87; Iraq conflict and, 89, 90–91; limits on right to use force, 61; nuclear arms and membership, 111–12; Resolution *338*, 35; resolution on Palestinian state, 52

United Nations Special Committee on Iraq (UNSCOM), 84

United States: bin Laden and, 10–11, 15; CIS states and, 73; coalition action against Iraq by, 59; cold war and, 14; criticism of unilateral security actions, 65–66; double standard on terrorism, 77; foreign oil dependence, 74; Georgian-Russian relations and, 127; on humanitarian interventions vs. preservation of UN mechanism, 63–64; investigation of September *11* attacks, 7–8; Iraqi Atomic Energy Commission and, 83; on Iraq and weapons monitoring, 87; joint statement on Middle East peace, 37; Kosovo Liberation Army and, 13; Libyan terrorism policies and, 5; Madrid Peace Conference and, 37–38; Middle East deadlock and, 51; Middle East peace process and, 31–32, 33–34; Middle East Quartet and, 55; multipolarity and, 97–98, 100–01; on NMD developments,

108; partial plan for Middle East peace, 35–36; public opinion on military action in Iraq, 88; Russia as potential partner, 135; Russian economic reforms and, 114–15; Russia's world role and, 132–35; scientific and technical production in, 97; space-based antimissile defense system plans, 105–06; strike against Iraq, 46–47; as superpower, 94–95; terrorism policies of, 4; UNSCOM weapons inspections in Iraq and, 84–85, 86; UN Security Council resolution on Palestinian state and, 52; use of force without UN auspices, 59, 61–62; Uzbekistan partnership, 71. *See also* Bush, George W.; Terrorism; *U.S. officials by name*
U.S.-Russia Strategic Offensive Reductions Treaty *(2002)*, 67

Unocal, 74
Uzbekistan, 69, 70, 71, 72–73

Vance, Cyrus, 36
Veselov, V. A., 100

Wahhabism, 27–28
Warsaw Pact, 94
Weapons of mass destruction (WMD), 15, 17, 84–85, 110–12. *See also* Nuclear weapons
Weizman, Ezer, 37
West Bank and Gaza, 48, 55–56
World Trade Organization, 117–18

Yugoslavia, 59, 61–63

Zahir Shah, Mohammad, 78, 81
Zasulich, Vera, 2
Zemin, Jiang, 71
Zubaydah, Abu, 16